Tributes to the
Life and Legacy of
BILL BRIGHT

FROM JULY 30, 2003, MEMORIAL SERVICE

"The thing I learned from him more than anything else is not how to dream or how to dare, but how to die. The last time I saw him, he was there in the bed, propped up with his telephone, commanding the world. And laying out vision, telling me, 'Adrian, here's what you need to do, here's what you ought to do, believe this, pray this, try this.'"

—Dr. Adrian Rogers
Senior Pastor, Bellevue Baptist Church, Cordova, Tennessee

"Bill Bright is the one who fully convinced me by his life that you can touch the whole world if you are willing to pay the price."

—Dr. Charles Stanley
Best-selling Author of *Finding Peace* and Senior Pastor,
First Baptist Church, Atlanta

"When I asked him how I could pray for him, his unhesitating question would be this, 'Bob, pray that I will never leave my first love.' His footprints even to the end lead to his first love. I said, 'Bill, what's the best thing that's happened to you today?' He said, 'I had a great phone call.' I said, 'Bill, who was it?' He said it was the President. I said, 'Bill, that's incredible.' With a pause and a slight chuckle he said, 'It was, it was an honor, but Bob, when you are preparing to meet Who I'm going to meet, even a call from the President fades by comparison.'"

—Dr. Robert E. Reccord
President, North American Mission Board, Southern Baptist Convention

"My life has been touched by him like the man in the Bible whose name was Barnabas, the son of encouragement. He encouraged me, he encouraged all of us. There was never a more faithful friend, or a greater servant of the Lord. I miss him terribly, and I thank God that he's with the Lord, but I almost wish that the Lord had just left him around a little bit more because he was such a blessing to all of us."

—Rev. Pat Robertson
Founder and Chairman, The Christian Broadcasting Network

"I'll never forget him sitting at that table when all of us were talking with these bright, profound theological thoughts, and Bill Bright was saying, 'I just want to stand before the Lord someday and not have failed to lead every single person I could to Christ.' That's courage. That's Bill Bright. That's the essence of the man. He had selflessness, which ought to be emulated by every single Christian servant and worker. He never put himself first."

—Charles W. Colson
Founder, Prison Fellowship Ministries

"The group had finished its work and it was about 5:30, and I said, 'before we close I'd like to just ask, Bill, are you on the line?' 'I'm here,' he said. 'I want you to know I'm here rejoicing in the name of my Lord and Savior, Jesus Christ.' He said, 'I'm always rejoicing.' I'll never forget that. That was his signature song."

—Tim Goeglein
Special Assistant to the President of the United States of America

"I think Bill Bright was one of the most focused people I ever knew. He had one goal in life, to share the good news of Jesus Christ with as many people as possible. And by every means possible. His vision, his single-mindedness and his dedication were a constant example to me and to countless others whose lives he touched across the world. He loved everybody, and I learned a great deal from him. Many times Bill would call me on the phone or come to see me just to encourage me in the work of the Lord. He always left me with a Scripture verse, and I knew he was always praying for me . . . The Great Commission has never been rescinded and the spiritual needs of the world have never been greater. May the memory of Bill's life challenge each of us to a deeper dedication to Christ and a greater zeal to spread His word to the ends of this earth as long as God gives us life."

—Billy Graham
World-Renowned Evangelist and Author

"Bill brought a sense of peace and hope. That in the midst of the sometimes crazy world, God still reigns . . . To know Bill Bright was to know God better. His very life was a sermon that inspired us all. He had that rare combination of great giftedness and even greater humility. Bill was an incredible visionary who changed his world. He lived by principle and practiced a practical walk with Christ that was both sensible and sincere. He was truly salt and light."

—U.S. Senator Elizabeth Dole
Former President of the American Red Cross

"Bill Bright is recognized all over the world by thoughtful men and women as one of the most influential, one of the greatest figures of the twentieth century, or for that matter, any century. Day after day, year after year, he expressed his confidence in Jesus Christ. That was the great certainty of his life . . . He had this phenomenal ability to see in people around him qualities of intellect and character and personality that we never knew we had. And in the process, from all over the world he attracted and brought around himself men and women of special intellect, special talents, special dedication, and idealism. What a movement he created."

—Former U.S. Senator William Armstrong

"Just a few days before he passed away, I went to his bedside and knelt beside him and I promised him that I would do my very best with a team of other very capable people to leave a tangible legacy for his life, so that men and women internationally could be raised up to be Christian leaders to stand in the gap to make a difference for God."

—John Maxwell
Founder of the INJOY Group, Chairman of the Board,
Global Pastors Network, and *New York Times* Best-Selling Author

From July 2003 Farewell Tribute *A Life Lived Well*

(Used by Permission of *Worldwide Challenge* Magazine)

"We have deeply appreciated the consistency and dedication of Bill and Vonette Bright, who have never wavered in their love and commitment to Jesus Christ. They have kept their lives above reproach and have been marvelous role models for us all."

—Shirley Dobson
Chairperson, National Day of Prayer

"During my term as president, I often said that there can be no definition of a successful life that does not include service to others. As founder and president of Campus Crusade for Christ, Bill Bright has done so much to show the invaluable beauty and importance of faith to countless devoted Christians. He truly is what I often refer to as 'one of a thousand points of light.'"

—George H. W. Bush
Former President of the United States of America

"A few months after 'Stand in the Gap: A Sacred Assembly of Men' in the fall of 1997, Promise Keepers faced serious financial stress. The entire staff had been put on volunteer status. We couldn't pay salaries and had to put all our energy into making the 1998 conference happen. That's when Dr. Bright called with an amazing offer. He wrote a letter to Campus Crusade supporters, and appealed to them on our behalf. We received hundreds of thousands of dollars in support at a critical time and never lost a step on making those conferences happen for men across the United States."

—Bill McCartney
Founder, Promise Keepers

"Bill not only was a proven, strong, internationally recognized leader in the Christian community, but a gentleman who exemplified personal integrity, living out moral values which governed his life."

—Ted W. Engstrom
Former President, World Vision

"Bill Bright's faith and desire to share Christ was so much on the forefront of his mind; he was so captivated by his calling to reach others for Christ that it became contagious. You simply couldn't be around Bill without walking away with a greater desire to share Christ. Many people, including myself, so often think of evangelism as a task to accomplish. But Bill never looked at it that way. To Bill, evangelism was just a way of life."

—Josh McDowell
Author of the bestseller *Evidence That Demands a Verdict*

"Bill Bright challenged me to think big and dream big and ask God for big things . . . Bill was the man who most influenced my life in another way—his incredibly close walk with the Lord. I had been with him in every kind of situation for forty-one years, and with Bill Bright it was always 'what you see is what you get.'"

—Dave Hannah
Chairman and CEO, Impact 1 Hundred and Founder, Athletes in Action

"Bill Bright believed in a big God, so he had big dreams and took big risks. God honored that faith over and over again. So much of Saddleback's ministry was shaped by the personal influence of my dear, dear friend, Bill Bright. Bill taught me that complete obedience, dependent faith, and simple tools can change the world. Millions of people now have faith in Christ because of *The Four Spiritual Laws,* the *Jesus* film, and *The Spirit-filled Life* booklet. In the early years of Saddleback, Bill was one of the few Christian leaders who understood our strategy, and I will always be grateful for his loving support and how he believed in me when I was just a kid. Bill Bright, along with Billy Graham, was one of the two Giants for God who towered over the 20th Century."

—Rick Warren
Pastor of Saddleback Church, Lake Forest, CA,
and author of *The Purpose-Driven Life*

THE
JOURNEY

Finishing with Joy

BILL
BRIGHT

Foreword by DR. JAMES C. DOBSON
Afterword by VONETTE ZACHARY BRIGHT

THOMAS NELSON PUBLISHERS®
Nashville

A Division of Thomas Nelson, Inc.

Published in Nashville, Tennessee, by Thomas Nelson, Inc.

ISBN 0-7852-6169-9

To my beloved Vonette,
lover, friend, partner in life and ministry,
with my deep gratitude, unending admiration,
and undying love.

Contents

ACKNOWLEDGMENTS

Friendship with the LORD *is reserved for those who fear him.*
With them he shares the secrets of his covenant.

—PSALM 25:14

*D*ying days have given me glorious new opportunities to enjoy the presence and power of God. I am very grateful to Sam Moore, president of Thomas Nelson, Inc. At various meetings in recent years, he insisted that I write this book. I also want to thank Executive Vice President and Group Publisher Michael Hyatt, Nelson Books Senior Vice President and Publisher Jonathan Merkh, Vice President and Editor in Chief Brian Hampton, Managing Editor Kyle Olund, and their staff who have been very helpful in making the manuscript ready for the press. More than ever I have benefited from the aid of my family, colleagues, and fellow staff who have helped with the many communications required in writing from my various beds, in hospitals and at home. I have received invaluable assistance from my biographer, Michael Richardson, whose book *Amazing Faith* was honored for writing excellence with the Gold Medallion Award. In this undertaking, most of all, I have experienced the faithfulness of our God who not only gives us His will but also promises to produce it in and through us. It is my earnest prayer that many will be drawn closer to our dear Lord and be able to see more clearly and experience more fully His wonderful love and joy as a result of this writing. All praise and glory must go to our great Creator-God and Savior, who alone is worthy.

FOREWORD

hat an honor it is to be asked by Mrs. Vonette Bright to write the foreword for this crowning book written by her beloved husband, Dr. Bill Bright, which was completed just three weeks before his death at eighty-one years of age. Although the board of directors of Focus on the Family, to whom I am accountable, established a firm policy many years ago that prohibited my agreeing to write forewords and endorsements, Vonette's request had to be seen as an exception. Indeed, Bill's life was exceptional in every regard. He was a giant among men.

There is no one I admired and loved more than Dr. Bright, who was perhaps the most influential Christian leader to live since the first century A.D. His passion for worldwide evangelism resulted in literally millions of people coming to personal relationships with Jesus Christ. By the time of his death, he had written more than one hundred books and booklets, several of which were actually composed during that last year when he was slowly and painfully losing his battle with a debilitating illness called pulmonary fibrosis. Despite these limitations, Dr. Bright told me that he experienced the most productive days of his life as he sat in a wheelchair struggling to breathe. Incredibly, fifteen books and related projects were completed during his final twenty-four months, when lesser men and women would have given up in despair. It is characteristic of Bill Bright to have used every remaining moment of his life in service to the Savior.

The ministry that Bill and Vonette started at UCLA in 1951, Campus Crusade for Christ, is now active in 190 countries, and consists of 26,000 staff members (and an additional 553,000 trained volunteers) who are deployed on campuses and in various settings around the world. The programs and initiatives that took shape in his fertile mind are of legendary proportion, including the *JESUS* film that has been seen by more than 5.5 billion people to date, and the "I Found It" campaign, which swept the globe in 1975. It brought millions more to Christ. Dr. Bright's more recent creation, an Internet outreach called "The Evangelism Toolbox," has had an unprecedented impact.

Bill would be embarrassed, of course, to read the words I have written in praise of his accomplishments. He was a humble man whose primary objective was to give Christ the glory in every circumstance. He often spoke of the self-denial required of those who would walk in the footsteps of the Savior. Jesus Himself said, "If anyone would come after me, he must deny himself and take up his cross and follow me" (Matt. 16:24). Bill took that admonition to heart. He simply had no interest in egotism or self-promotion. He considered them to be a complete waste of time.

Dr. Bright also wasted no energy worrying about his approaching death. That became apparent when I invited him and Dr. Brandt Gustavson to be guests on our radio broadcast, which we entitled, "A Race to Heaven." Both of them knew that they were dying. Indeed, Dr. Gustavson made the crossing just five days later. Dr. Bright spoke candidly during our discussion about his illness. This is how his physician told him he would soon leave this earth. Bill said:

He sat me down one day—Vonette and me—in his office and said, "You don't seem to realize what's happening to you. You're dying. It's worse than cancer. It's worse than heart trouble. We can deal with these in some measure, but nobody can help you with pulmonary fibrosis. You are going to die a miserable death. You need to get your head out of the sand and be prepared for it."

So I said, "Well, praise the Lord. I'll see the Lord sooner than I'd planned."

My wife, Shirley, and I attended the deeply moving celebration of his home going held in Orlando, Florida. Vonette asked me and several other friends to say a few words on that day. From start to finish, the service was a testimony both to God's goodness and to Bill's humility. As it ended, and several thousand people made their way out of the church, I said to Shirley, "Please remember what happened on this day. The chances are great that you will outlive me. If that is the case, I want my memorial service to be modeled after the one we have just witnessed. Everything said and done served to lift up the lordship of Jesus Christ." Dr. Bright's long and distinguished list of accomplishments could have taken days for us to review and laud. Instead, there was hardly a comment made that praised or elevated this great man. It was befitting of one who had lived his life in humility and service to the Lord.

Dr. Bright had an enormous impact on me, personally. He was a role model and a father figure to me after my own dad passed away. In the 1980s, he was one of the most prominent Christian leaders in the world and had an international schedule that would have exhausted a globe-hopping Secretary of State. Despite the extreme demands placed on his time, he would periodically call to encourage and to pray with me.

Then in 1989, Focus on the Family and I were sued by a former employee for simply trying to defend one of the moral principles in which we believed. The situation was unfair and unjust, and I had grown increasingly agitated about being dragged into court. Bill heard about our plight and called once again to offer his support. He urged me to maintain a Christlike spirit and to avoid becoming bitter over the conflict. "Jim, let the Lord handle it for you," he said. And then, predictably, he asked if he could pray for me. I was humbled—not only by his intense personal interest in our situation, but by his desire to help me focus my energies on the Lord rather than on fuming over my circumstances. In so doing, he modeled for me how to find peace in the midst of adversity.

That ability to live above his circumstances exemplifies Dr. Bill Bright's lifelong approach to adversity. Only three days before his passing,

Shirley and I called Vonette from Europe, where we were enjoying a long-anticipated vacation. Word had reached us that Bill's health was deteriorating rapidly. We wanted to ask for an update on his condition and to assure the Brights of our prayers. We talked to Vonette for a few minutes, and then she said unexpectedly, "Bill is listening to you right now. He wants to talk to you."

When he joined us on the speaker phone that night, it was obvious to Shirley and me that our great friend would soon leave this world. His voice was raspy and weak, and his breathing was labored. He was straining for every syllable. As a result, we couldn't discern much of what Bill was trying to say. Nevertheless, I heard him utter two unmistakable phrases. He said, "I'm rejoicing," and then, "I love you." Imagine! This godly man was only three days away from the end of his earthly journey, yet he was praising God for His goodness and mercy. There was no hint of self-pity in his voice. It would have been perfectly reasonable for him to have complained or to have expressed anger over his difficult circumstances. But his last words to us this side of heaven were of his dependence on God and of his love for his friends. That was Bill Bright.

Words are not adequate to describe this great man or the impact he had on me and millions of others around the world. Yes, he was a loving husband who, along with his dear Vonette, maintained an exemplary Christian marriage to a watching world. He never compromised the standards of holiness that he determined to achieve as a young Christian. He was a loving father and grandfather. He was an admired leader of one of the world's most respected ministries. He was a good man, a kind man, and a generous man. Above all, he called himself "a slave of Jesus Christ." And, he was my very good friend. If you want to know more about the man, read on and let him speak for himself in this book. I'm sure you will catch the essence of one who, facing terminal illness and death, was eagerly anticipating his first face-to-face meeting with his Savior. He referred to that encounter as "the most glorious worship service of all time" (p. 155). He talked about that moment in our final radio broadcast when he said with excitement, "I will kneel in His presence—my Master, my Savior, my Lord, my King—and worship and adore and praise Him, for He is God. Apart from Him, life wouldn't even be worth living."

Bill Bright was brimming with joy on the eve of his death—and now that he has made the journey home, his cup is overflowing. He is gone, but I can still hear his final words ringing in my ears.

"I'm rejoicing," and "I love you."

Vonette, you are a great lady. You stood by your husband through pressures and responsibilities that must have been grueling at times. You were Bill's companion, his lover, and his colaborer for Christ. Thank you for keeping your testimony unspoiled and for maintaining steadfast love and devotion as a wife and mother. You have been an inspiration to Shirley and me. Thank you for your pivotal role in creating a specific observance each year for the National Day of Prayer, which would not exist in its present form without your diligence. There is a "crown of righteousness" awaiting you on that resurrection morning, when you and Bill will be reunited forever in the presence of the King. Shirley and I will be there too, through no merit of our own, along with a vast assembly of saints who remained faithful because of your ministry. That is the greatest legacy of all.

—**James C. Dobson, Ph.D.**
Founder and Chairman, Focus on the Family
October 2003

PREFACE

I have been asked if I have any last words before God calls me to a new assignment, and I do.

To my family, I pray that you will continue to love God with all your hearts, souls, minds, and strength; to obey His commandments; to trust His promises; to always seek first His kingdom; and to take the initiative to see that every member of the family, generation after generation, is encouraged to receive and follow our gracious Savior.

To the believing world, I would add this: in light of our failure through the years to be salt and light, as Jesus commanded, our generation is faced with a grave crisis. Anti-God forces have largely become the dominant voice and the major influence in our culture. My challenge to believers would be: reverse this tide. It is not enough to say, "I must live a godly life"—that is a given. It is not enough to say, "I must be a witness for Christ"—that is a given. Beyond these two, we must be salt and light in our culture, helping people to realize that the God of the Bible is our only hope.

To the unbelieving world, I say, First, every person follows someone. And my admonition would be: if you are going to follow anyone, follow Jesus of Nazareth, who changed the course of history. Most knowledgeable people believe Him to be the greatest person who ever lived. Second, everybody has a basic belief in something, a manual for living, even if it is something he or she invented. And if you are going to base your life on anything, base it on the authority of holy Scriptures. There is no book ever written that has the power to change lives like the Holy Bible, and there is no philosophy of men that can compare with the words of our Creator-God and Savior Jesus. The Bible is more important than all the books in all the libraries in the world.

With the apostle Paul,

I want you to know how much I have agonized for you . . . and for many other friends who have never known me personally. My goal is that they will be encouraged and knit together by strong ties of love. I want them to have full confidence because they have complete understanding of God's secret plan, which is Christ himself. In him lie hidden all the treasures of wisdom and knowledge . . . For in Christ the fullness of God lives in a human body, and you are complete through your union with Christ. He is the Lord over every ruler and authority in the universe. (Col. 2:1–3, 9–10)

I have been asked how I want to be remembered. The answer is: I want to be remembered as a slave of Jesus—nothing more, nothing less. Slaves need neither monuments nor recognition. They merely follow the example of our Lord (Phil. 2:7), of the apostle Paul (Rom. 1:1), and of Jesus' disciples, James (James 1:1), Peter (1 Peter 1:1), Jude (Jude 1), and others.

My life has been unbelievable, fantastic, beyond description, joyful, exciting, and adventuresome; words are inadequate to express my deep gratitude to God for His grace and blessings. My life has been far from perfect, of course. Insensitivity, preoccupation with the task at the expense of tender hearts, words unfitly spoken, the ego placed on the throne of my life where only Jesus belongs—who could list them all? But even my imperfections, my failures, my shortcomings have been worked together by God to bring blessing and fruitful ministry. Vonette and I often pinch ourselves and rejoice over how fortunate we are to be a part of something so magnificent as knowing our God, who created the universe, and loving and serving Him, trusting and obeying Him. He is awesome.

June 23, 2003
Orlando, Florida

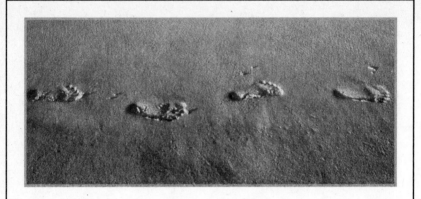

"Footprints in the Sand"

One night a man had a dream. He dreamed he was walking along the beach with the Lord. Across the sky flashed scenes from his life. For each scene, he noticed two sets of footprints in the sand: one belonged to him and the other to the Lord.

When the last scene of his life flashed before him, he looked back at the footprints in the sand. He noticed that many times along the path of his life there was only one set of footprints. He also noticed that it happened at the very lowest and saddest times in his life.

This really bothered him, and he questioned the Lord about it. "Lord, you said that once I decided to follow you, you'd walk with me all the way. But I have noticed that during the most troublesome times in my life, there is only one set of footprints. I don't understand why when I needed you most, you would leave me."

The Lord replied, "My precious, precious child, I love you, and I would never leave you. During your times of trial and suffering, when you see only one set of footprints, it was then that I carried you."

—Mary Stevenson

GOING HOME

I am like a person going on a journey in a stage coach,
who expects its arrival every hour, and is frequently looking
out the window for it . . . I am packed and sealed
and ready for the post.

—JOHN NEWTON, WRITER OF "AMAZING GRACE"

My dear fellow traveler,

Let me invite you to imagine us walking together for a while. I have been reflecting on the journey God has given me, and He has put it in my heart to share with someone like you some of the most meaningful lessons on the path, whether you are like me, near the journey's end, or whether you are beginning the walk with our Lord Jesus. They say hindsight is 20/20. If that is the case, my prayer is that we can share what I have discovered matters most about life.

When I think of a thoughtful walk, I think of a beach. I especially think of that wonderful poem "Footprints in the Sand." It notes that God walks beside us at all times, and when we see only one set of footprints, He has not left us but then begins to carry us. I am sensing that today as I write.

When you walk a beach, do you prefer sunrises or sunsets? For most of our ministry years, Vonette and I lived on the Pacific Coast, and when we occasionally got the opportunity, we walked along those California beaches to enjoy magnificent sunsets. They have always had a settling effect on me, calming and cooling from the heat of the day. In recent years, since we moved to Florida, friends have invited us to their homes on the Atlantic Ocean—and we have been blessed with the joy of sunrises. They have a stirring effect on me as the sun rises and brightens my whole being. So whether I look to the sunsets of the past years or to the sunrises of recent years, I see God's handiwork, and it is a joy to behold.

I have started this kind of reflecting for two reasons: first, we have taken the time to slow down enough to give real notice to sunsets and sunrises, and second, I have been hit with the certainty that I am in the grips of *terminal illness*. Have you ever thought that to be a strange term? When we get right down to it, our lives are locked into a *terminal* ending from their beginning. Scriptures suggest that God rather intends three-score and ten years for us, but we know from the beginning that it will end soon enough. I am not sure why hearing something specific from a physician makes *terminal* seem more final, but it does that.

One thing for sure, whether I draw from memories of sunsets or sunrises, from the East Coast or the West Coast, hearing that I had "less than six months to live" focused my attention on what is important and what is not. That is what the doctor told me in February 2003. From this vantage point, it is clear that only two things in this life really matter: (1) our health, and (2) the assurance of our salvation. Next to the Lord, of course, I prize my family and love them dearly, along with many wonderful friends and fellow staff. But everything else, especially material things, no longer hold my interest. One of the many benefits of being a slave of Jesus is that I own very little of this world's goods, so I do not have to be harried about what to do with wealth and lands. However, I go with the assurance that our great God and Savior will care for Vonette and our other family loved ones and the worldwide staff He has given Campus Crusade for Christ International. He has faithfully cared for us since its founding in 1951 when only Vonette and I were the staff. He is doing so today as there are more than 26,000 full-time staff and more than 225,000 associate staff operating in 191 nations and territories of the earth.

Most of my life I have associated living and dying with certain couplets of truth: "Only one life, 'twill soon be past, only what's done for Christ will last," and "Life is short, death is sure; sin is a curse and Christ is the cure." (That is another thing about the perspective I now enjoy: I respect all the profound theological propositions one can, and probably should, absorb; but right now, if it does not pertain plainly to life or death, heaven or hell, and the fulfillment of the Great Commission, my interest is short-lived.) I am more concerned than ever with those who are lost in this world without the knowledge of Christ. I am more committed than ever to doing all I can for as long

> *I never had to walk the last mile alone.*

as I can to share with as many as I can the awesome love of our great Creator-God and Savior. During two hospitalizations recently, I had the privilege of witnessing and praying with two nurses, three aides, one orderly and one physician. What joy, great joy, as my spirit sang with the chorus writer Kurt Kaiser, "Oh, how He loves you and me."

THE WALK HOME

I was born and grew up on a ranch five miles from the small community of Coweta, Oklahoma, so walking was central to my youth. A school bus took me to classes each day, but I often had sports practice or a drama rehearsal, and that meant walking five miles home. The fall of darkness made the journey seem longer, but my loving mother would always meet me one mile from our home. I never had to walk the last mile alone. Just the knowledge of her presence turned that part of the journey into something positive I looked forward to.

It was strategic for me, even as a teenager, because that last mile included a spooky hollow and a creek, trees bending in the wind, and a hoot owl whose mission in life was to raise the hair on the back of my neck.

About a quarter mile from our house, I could see the light from home. It always buoyed my spirit and put strength in my pace. The light meant warmth around a big natural gas heating unit that circulated heat throughout the ranch house. And, regardless of my particular state of affairs that day, it meant my father and the rest of our family soon would welcome me.

At this point, you and most believers are ahead of me. You know that this real-life experience portrays how I feel about closing my journey on this earth. I am on the last mile, but I am not alone. The Lord Jesus by His Holy Spirit is with me, and the knowledge of His presence dispels the darkness and allays any fears. We have tender conversations. I can see the light of my real home, heaven, and it beckons and buoys me more than ever, the nearer I draw to it. It is a glorious sight. My precious heavenly Father and loved ones in the great family of God are open-armed, and I can barely wait to get home at last.

Dear friend, I do want to say it matters whether you walk alone. It matters that you have Jesus in your heart guiding you. It matters whether heaven is your home. It matters that you know the heavenly Father and, more, that He knows you personally. Please don't take the next step, much less the last mile, without Him in your heart. Please see the Appendix of this book to learn how, if you died today, you could spend eternity with our blessed Lord in heaven.

Please don't take the next step, much less the last mile, without Him in your heart.

Recently on the journey, I have been asked what it was like to "hear the bad news," but I must tell you I did not think of it that way. Hard news? Yes. Bad news? Not really. Let me explain.

RECOIL OR REJOICE

My first wake-up call to the possibility of terminal disease came with the diagnosis of prostate cancer in 1993. Then in 1998 I became aware that my incurable disease, pulmonary fibrosis, had begun its stranglehold on my lungs. Diabetes attacked me in 2001. Naturally, I have been asked, How do God's people handle the "bad news" of disease and death? My reply is that they meet it with the good news of life in Jesus Christ, the Lord of all and all time. Jesus taught us to expect troubles in this life and also to overcome them through faith in Him. As for death, He has promised that anyone believing in Him would never die eternally, although the flesh would wither and pass away. So the real question for me was: Would I recoil in denial and frustration, questioning God, or would I be obedient and thank and praise Him for this new opportunity to know Him better? Would I continue to love, trust, and obey my dear Lord and His Word until my last breath?

I remember the only other season of serious illness in my life. In my youth I spent a few days in the hospital for an appendectomy and a tonsillectomy. Even with all my worldwide travel, I can remember having nothing more serious than one or two bouts with dysentery and an occasional cold. But in 1983 I went into the hospital for a hernia operation. It was then I realized that we should never take good health for granted. Perhaps we all need to be sick or to face some kind of adversity occasionally, so that we will stop and count our many blessings, especially those of good health.

It has been my joy to spend fifty-eight years helping people to experience and live well the abundant life in Jesus Christ. It is now my desire, with God's enabling, to help people live and die well with the assurance of everlasting life in Jesus Christ. Both challenges give us the opportunity to rejoice in faith or recoil in fear. God leaves that up to us.

A friend of mine was stricken with a life-changing disease, and he called his son to report. The son, a pastor and a Bible scholar, offered a brief consolation but poignantly added, "So, Dad, it looks like you're going to have a chance to walk your faith here."

Perhaps that is what I am doing, walking the path of pain with pockets full of promises from God. Then, too, a certain question of integrity arises: How many times have I advised others that God is faithful, His Word is true, and His Spirit's power can cause believers to soar where others can only flutter? Will I practice what I preached?

Recently, our wonderful friend Leroy Eger reminded me of a time years ago when his mother was dying and he asked me to visit her. As I did, he will not let me forget, I counseled her with words such as these: "Beloved, the day you were born, God knew the day you will die. He created you. He loves you. He died for you, and He was raised from the dead and now lives in your heart. He is waiting to welcome you to your heavenly home. There is nothing you can do about this except trust Him because He has everything under control."

Leroy called me later to remind me: "Remember what you told my mother." Isn't that great?

By God's enabling until now, I have—every day, every hour, every breath—an opportunity to let His truth govern and make possible my behavior. My mind has reasoned this way: When Jesus was under attack (tested by Satan), what did He do? He quoted Scripture to each challenge, and He experienced victory. Jesus now lives in me. So by faith and through the assurance of His Word, I can experience supernatural joy, peace, and victory too.[1]

Believers are commanded to meet trials with joy and thanksgiving. James said, "Dear brothers and sisters, whenever trouble comes your way, let it be an opportunity for joy" (James 1:2). Paul told the Romans, "We can rejoice, too, when we run into problems and trials, for we know that they are good for us—they help us learn to endure" (Rom. 5:3). And Paul instructed those in Greece: "Always be joyful. Keep on praying. No matter what happens, always be thankful, for this is God's will for you who belong to Christ Jesus" (1 Thess. 5:16–18).

Please understand, I am trying to be neither brave nor preachy—just obedient. By God's gracious power within, I do intend with all my heart to face the winter season of my life on earth in this way: full of faith in our great Creator-God and Savior, full of joy in the truth of His promises, full of peace about my future that the Prince of Peace holds in His hands.

"WORSE THAN CANCER"

So I was reasonably prepared when the physician told me I would die a terrible death with an incurable disease. He said it would be worse than a heart attack or cancer: "You will choke to death." Aloud, in his office, I replied, "Thank You, Lord." The specialist was taken aback. Even though he was a longtime friend, he rebuked me because he did not believe I was really listening to his comments. "You don't understand," he said, restating the horrors of dying by suffocation because of pulmonary fibrosis. I said, "I believe the Bible, and it says Christians are to give thanks in *all* things and to rejoice whatever the news." The doctor remained disapproving of my response, perhaps thinking I was in denial. No, I was in declaration of the truth of God's word and will for my life. And with His help I will continue to declare His faithfulness as long as I live on this earth.

In late 2000 Vonette and I returned to Arrowhead Springs after I had extensive testing and treatments from three of the most highly reputed pulmonary institutions in the country. The physicians gave me no hope. One hospital staff did give me excruciating pain as a result of a biopsy of my lungs. They offered experimental drugs, but Vonette and I decided against them.

Vonette recalled the scene: "When we first learned that Bill had pulmonary fibrosis, we both went to our knees to pray, and as we were praying, we thanked the Lord for all the years we had enjoyed together and the phenomenal ministry He had given us. And when you have lived fifty-four years together, that's the pinnacle of everything. Anything more than fifty years is just God's grace and joy. We decided we are not going to have any regrets. We have had a marvelous journey together with our dear Lord. We have done what we thought God wanted us to do during the last two years, even though Bill has lived on oxygen twenty-four hours each day and been bedridden for several months."

I remember vividly the fall of 2000 while we were in California. I decided that I did not want to return in a box, so we discussed returning to our home in Florida. I reflected on the Word of God and the example of the patriarchs as they were passing from this life. Their practice was to call a family assembly and pray a prayer of blessing upon the heads of their descendants, believing God to provide them with something more precious than worldly materials.

Realizing that I would not likely see our California family again, I saw clearly what I should do. Vonette and I met with our son Zac, a Presbyterian pastor, and his wife, Terry, and their children Rebecca Dawn and Christopher Zachary. As we gathered, I laid my hands upon each one and prayed a special prayer of blessing, consecrating their lives to our great Creator-God and our Savior, Jesus Christ, asking an anointing from God Himself for each one, expecting God to use them for His glory. It was a very moving and meaningful experience for all of us, especially for me.

PREPARATION

From that point on, all I had to do was face the obvious facts. Even under normal circumstances, any mortality table says it is most likely that a husband will die before his wife. National data show that 80 percent of people die in a hospital or a similar institution, even though the same number want to die at home. Meanwhile, if a man loves his wife as Christ loves the church, he will anticipate her needs and prepare for them (Eph. 5:25).

Death is like a college exam. It is not the final exam—that is when we stand before God in the Day of Judgment. But it is a test, and as for any test, we should prepare for it. Our preparation, in fact, will go a long way toward determining how we respond when the test comes.

So Vonette and I prepared. Salvation is the first issue, about which everyone must be sure. On what basis do I expect God to invite me into His heaven? On the basis of the shed blood of Jesus upon the cross of Calvary for my sin, nothing more, nothing less. I am fully aware that salvation is a gift of God that I receive by faith alone, but I am also aware that if good works do not follow, I am disobedient (Eph. 2:8–10). All believers are called to be "salt and light" in their society.

WHY NOT A MIRACLE?

When I first heard that I was living with a terminal disease, I had to decide whether merely to accept it or to seek God's divine healing. As the time passed and Vonette and I sought God's will, we reached the decision: we would do both. Yes, I can accept the life sentence of terminal disease as permitted by God, but I also believe God is able to heal, and by faith, I believed I should have an attitude to seek His healing.

God does heal. Physicians and surgeons can help. Cancer can be beaten; just ask New York Yankees Manager Joe Torre, hockey star Mario Lemieux, and the outstanding international cyclist Lance Armstrong.

Faced with cancer, they sought healing, and it came. But not everyone is healed with extended life on this earth. Why is that? Why do some receive healing and others die? Our sovereign God has the answer in His will and His timing, and I trust Him. His ways are perfect.

Jim Valvano, head basketball coach at North Carolina State, was stricken with cancer in the 1980s, but he didn't sit on his hands. While dying, he became a champion for fund-raising to support cancer research. He also became an inspirational leader with the message: "Never give up." He was irrepressible. He would not slow down, much less stop. "You have to have enthusiasm for life," he said, "and you have to have a goal."

In following the Lord Jesus, I have discovered we do not have to make up a goal or manufacture a purpose. The enthusiasm (literally, *en theos*, "in God") comes from knowing the Lord Jesus and His indwelling Holy Spirit. The goal, for believers, always is to bring glory to the Lord God. Jesus faced the critics who met the boy blind since birth and stopped their mouths by saying, in effect: "Stop criticizing. This has not happened to him because he or his parents have sinned; this has happened to him that God might be glorified." I'll tell you more about my experience with this in Chapter 2.

HEADING HOME

Vonette and I to this day continue to pray for my healing and accept the fact that the Lord can take me through the valley of death any time He wishes. Rather than staying frozen on that issue, we decided to move on with life. We made the decision to be buried in Florida beside each other with a single common headstone that says, "William R. (Bill) and Vonette Zachary Bright—Slaves of Jesus." This term, *slaves of Jesus*, causes some to pause, but it is essential to who we are. We think of Philippians 2:7, which describes Jesus, the very Son of God, coming to earth disguised as a slave. The apostle Paul, in Romans 1:1, Romans 6, and other passages, indicated he considered himself a slave of Jesus Christ. Peter, James, and Jude also viewed themselves this way (2 Peter 1:1; James 1:1; Jude 1).

I know my last breath is something to look forward to because the next breath after that one I will draw in the awesome glory of my precious Savior and almighty God in the celestial air of heaven. I join with Paul in saying, "We are of good courage . . . and prefer rather to be absent from the body and to be at home with the Lord. Therefore also we have as our ambition, whether at home or absent, to be pleasing to Him" (2 Cor. 5:8–9 NASB).

Our beloved Lord is our example in all things, and what was His attitude as He approached His mission to die for us? "And it came to pass, when the time was come that he should be received up, he stedfastly set his face to go to Jerusalem" (Luke 9:51 KJV). He faced it squarely. He did not shy away from the task.

With a grateful heart to God, who has the final word in these matters, I can say these diseases have liberated me to focus on some of the most important and exciting projects of my entire life, in a new and fresh walk with our Lord. I am rejoicing.

During the last fifty years, I have traveled many millions of miles ministering to our staff and their disciples, students, and laymen in most countries of the world. Through the years I have experienced the truth that God is real, His promises are true, time on earth is an exciting but brief adventure, and heaven is my home. Without question it has been a joyous journey.

There is a longing in every human heart for some place to call home. According to their circumstances, people may try to make their dwelling places on earth as heavenly as possible—safe, bright, arrayed with vistas, full of love and peace. For the follower of Jesus, heaven is the home where when you come knowing Jesus Christ as Lord and Savior, the heavenly Father God greets you, and because of His faithfulness to His promises, you can be assured that you will be admitted.

God is real, His promises are true, time on earth is an exciting but brief adventure, and heaven is my home. Without question it has been a joyous journey.

I want to be faithful to my last breath, praising Him and rejoicing as I go, and I have at least four reasons: (1) because of who He is; (2) because of all He has done and is doing for me; (3) because it is right, according to the Word of God, as I have indicated; and (4) because there is an eternal formula: as you sow, so shall you reap (Gal. 6:8). As you give, you will receive. If you live in love, you will experience the fruit of love accordingly.

I am praying to be healed that my Lord would be glorified, as I feel the Holy Spirit has prompted me to pray. But I am also ready to go. I am expecting to be ushered into the place of majestic beauty that is heaven. Mark me down as ready to go, ready to stay, ready His will to do. Mine is a win-win experience. I win when I die and go to be with the Lord, or I win if I continue to live and serve Him and others. In either case, I want to live or die for the glory of God.

Victor Hugo in his old age said, "When I go down to the grave, I can say, 'I have finished my day's work,' but I cannot say, 'I have finished my life's work' . . . The tomb is not a blind alley; it is an open thoroughfare . . . The tomb, which closes on the dead, opens the firmament. And that what on earth we call the end is the commencement. Death is the portal of life."[2]

My confidence is in His holy, inspired Word, which alone gives comfort as we face death. For example, one Sunday morning, English preacher Charles Haddon Spurgeon, known for teaching directly from passages of Scripture, stood at the pulpit and left the Bible closed. "Some have found fault with me," he said, "contending that I am too old-fashioned. I am always quoting the Bible and do not say enough about science. Well, there's a poor widow here who has lost her only son. She wants to know if she will ever see him again. Let's turn to science for the answer: Will she see him? Where is he? Does death end all?"

There was a long pause. "We are waiting for an answer," he said. "This woman is anxious." Another long pause. "Nothing to say? Then we'll turn to the Book!" Spurgeon then began to cite the joyous promises of God about heaven and the assurance that believers have in Christ.

We can think of crossing the threshold of death into heaven in this way: let us say a baby in the womb enjoys a perfectly delightful environment. Its needs are completely met, and it has little to distract it. But when the time comes for it to be born into this world—to enter another dimension of existence—it protests with screams. However, before long, usually surrounded with much love and tender care, it adjusts to this life and grows and develops more as it is surrounded with love and nurture. So it is when the time comes for us.

We all can profit from this actual sign at a Georgia church: "God always promises a soft landing; but He never promised a smooth flight." As truth is better than fiction, the church is located on Loving Road. That is the path reflecting God's wonderful plan for our lives.

"How Great Thou Art"

O Lord my God! When I in awesome wonder
Consider all the worlds Thy hands have made;
I see the stars, I hear the rolling thunder,
Thy pow'r throughout the universe displayed:

Then sings my soul, my Savior God, to Thee,
HOW GREAT THOU ART! HOW GREAT THOU ART!
Then sings my soul, my Savior God, to Thee,
HOW GREAT THOU ART! HOW GREAT THOU ART!

—Stuart K. Hine

TWO

A CLEAR PERSPECTIVE

For just as the heavens are higher than the earth,
so are my ways higher than your ways and
my thoughts higher than your thoughts.

—GOD (ISA. 55:9)

*I*sn't it sharpening to mind and soul to prepare for a long journey? It makes you ask, "What really matters most?" Countless times as I have traveled many millions of miles around the world in ministry, I had to be sure there were plans for my family in the event I did not return. In effect, you have to take your life apart and put it together without you in it. Important issues arise such as selecting a "personal representative" to help in family decisions in your absence.

Every member of any nation's military goes through this as he or she is ordered to deploy. No one ever handled this process better than 2003 *Columbia* space shuttle commander Rick Husband, a follower of Jesus. According to news reports, as he planned for what turned out to be his last trip into space, he made a series of sixteen videotapes for his wife and children, one for each day of his scheduled mission. In one of them he said, "We never know what the next day will hold for us . . . Grasp life with all your might, hold tight to the ones you love, and live life as though there were no tomorrow." Then in another tape, he anticipated the possibility that he might not return and advised them: "Tears will fall and your heart will bear the burden of pain, but God's love will see you through. I've walked the steps to Heaven and am with God now, be comforted in knowing He will take care of me."

What a glorious witness to our great Creator-God and Savior! But, you may ask, where did he get a perspective such as that? Did he invent it? No, his videotapes were a result of his own studies of the Bible. He anticipated painful times by knowing the Word of God. He surely must have read of Jesus' command to seek first the kingdom of God and all other needs would be provided (Matt. 6:33), and in the very next verse He urged, "So don't worry about tomorrow, for tomorrow will bring its own worries. Today's trouble is enough for today." I personally think those two commands go together in this way: if you are worrying about tomorrow, you are not seeking to put first the kingdom of God today; and if you do seek first His kingdom, you will be so focused on Him that you will not be found worrying about tomorrow.

> *Seeing difficulty through the eyes of God is the only way I can comprehend anyone coping sensibly with death and dying.*

Seeing difficulty through the eyes of God is the only way I can comprehend anyone coping sensibly with death and dying. It takes His perspective, and He says, "Count it all joy" when you have problems and trials (James 1:2 NKJV). So I decided to receive the "bad news" of the medical reports as a gift from God. Yes, a gift. What do you do with a gift?

Receive it, even clutch it to yourself.

Thank the Giver, even before understanding the gift.

Open it and discover what the Giver has in store for you.

Begin to employ and enjoy the gift.

That is how it has been for me and the terminal illness of pulmonary fibrosis. For more than two years I have been on oxygen twenty-four hours each day, when I am sleeping, when I am showering, and when I am videotaping, which in the last few months has been while I am confined to a bed. I view this privilege as one of the greatest gifts of my life because it has drawn me to an even deeper intimacy with our Lord, and because it has stirred me to more faith and service to our awesome God.

George Mueller, a man of tremendous faith who cared for hundreds of orphans in England entirely by prayer, once said, "God delights to increase the faith of His children. We ought, instead of wanting no trials before victory, no exercise for patience, to be willing to take them from God's hand as a means. I say—and say it deliberately—trials, obstacles, difficulties, and sometimes defeats, are the very food of faith."

Paul commended the Thessalonians for their attitude of receiving harsh times as a gift: "So you received the message with joy from the Holy Spirit in spite of the severe suffering it brought you. In this way, you imitated both us and the Lord" (1 Thess. 1:6).

Paul said, "Even if my life is to be poured out like a drink offering to complete the sacrifice of your faithful service (that is, if I am to die for you), I will rejoice, and I want to share my joy with all of you. And you should be happy about this and rejoice with me" (Phil. 2:17–18)

From the beginning of this journey home, I fully embraced God's perspective about my illness, pain, and discomfort. Again, I am not saying that I somehow cavalierly denied or dismissed the pain and suffering. I am merely seeking to agree with God on how to look at the challenge. It is an "attitude check" if ever there were one. And an attitude of gratitude to our great Creator-God and Savior always demonstrates faith and pleases God.

GOD PROVIDES IN WHAT GOD PERMITS

Dying is no fun, but it can be a fantastic experience. I believe God never allows anything to happen to followers of Christ, His children, that is not filtered through His love and refined for our good and His glory. Nothing can separate us from His love—neither life, nor death—so we remain enveloped in His loving care, no matter our physical circumstances.[1] He may not intend the diabetes, the cancer, and the pulmonary fibrosis that eat at my life, but they are, for Him, relatively minor matters that He has allowed to come my way. His very name is Jehovah-jireh (the Lord provides), so I can conclude that He will provide for me in what He has permitted to enter my life. Dying is just another opportunity to trust our wonderful Lord. It is comforting to say with Martin Luther: "Though I know not the way He leads me, well do I know my Guide."

Please do not think of me as being casual about dying as a Pollyanna or as the escapee from an asylum. The pains and sorrows of life and of death are no merry-go-round ride. Do I hurt? Yes. Do I sense suffering? Certainly. Do I wish my beloved wife, Vonette, our sons, their wives, our grandchildren, and my dear fellow staff did not have to go through this experience? Yes, although I would not want them to miss any of it if it is His will for their lives. The point is that every life includes periods of anguish, regret, grief and loss, suffering and lament. Why should the end of physical life on earth be any different?

> *In any case, I do not need to feel good or be ecstatic in order to be in the center of God's will.*

In any case, I do not need to feel good or be ecstatic in order to be in the center of God's will. He did not promise feelings of exuberance while passing through the shadow of death; He promised His presence and the absolute absence of fear.[2] And He is faithful to keep His word although everyone else may not keep theirs.

What about miracles? I have seldom experienced thunder and lightning, as did Elijah or Paul. But I have been experiencing what are miracles to me. Let me mention two. First—and I believe this has happened because of persistence in prayer by Vonette and many others—God has extended my life. Second, a marvelous miracle for me has been the way Vonette has joined me in thanking God for what has come upon us. I have asked her to tell of this work of God in her life.

VONETTE'S INSIGHTS

Vonette said, "There have been many passages of Scripture God has used to minister to me. One of the most meaningful is John 14:28, where Jesus says, 'Remember what I told you: I am going away, but I will come back to you again. If you really love me, you will be very happy for me, because now I can go to the Father.' God took a huge lump out of my heart with that insight. I do 'really love' Bill, so I had to agree that I should be 'very happy' for him when he goes to the Father. And, of course, it reflected the very attitude that Bill kept showing to me. Also, I had seen in the life of a dear friend, Ida Morris, such an amazing radiance at the passing of her husband, Allen. I remember taking her aside and saying, 'Ida, tell me, really, how are you? You seem so radiant.' She replied, 'Vonette, really I am so joyful for Allen that I feel guilty.'

"Actually, I thought her attitude might fade, but it has not. Then when I found this source of joy in John 14:28, I told her: 'Ida, I know where you got this assurance of joy.' And she said she had never heard of the passage. Shortly after, Bill and I attended the Billy Graham-sponsored Amsterdam 2000 conference on evangelism, which drew ten thousand persons. Bill was on oxygen, and people were asking me about his health. I shared with them that verse, and they, too, had not seen it that way.

"Another discovery God gave me helped with our natural desire to know when something is going to happen, even though we know we should simply trust God about matters of timing. But God knew my need, and He gave me an answer to that while I was reading the New Living Translation version of John 14:3: 'When everything is ready, I will come to get you, so that you will always be with me where I am.'

"What a blessing to know our times are in His hands, and when He is ready—and not before—Jesus will come for us. I continue to pray Bill will be with us many more years, but I trust God whatever the timing.

"In the meantime God is doing a new thing in our lives. I do not believe God would permit the breakup of a family unless He has something more for the surviving spouse to do. So I expect to continue in ministry, in writing and speaking and leading, as God gives opportunity."

I praise God for the insights He has given Vonette and for her trust in and obedience to our Lord and His living Word. It has thrilled me that our sons Zac and Brad and their families have reached similar decisions because they know the same Creator-God and Savior—a sovereign Lord, a loving Father, a tender Comforter. So have many of our friends and fellow staff. This is what dying is all about: with Him, it is a joyful walk into the gates of heaven in a blessed assurance that He goes with me; without Him, it is a cringing, fearful shrinking from eternal separation from God. Our family members have learned that our relations with God must be fueled by faith. This is what He requires. Without faith we cannot please Him. In fact, whatever is not of faith is sin in His eyes. Our only means of living in Him is by faith, so trusting Him to see us through any and all trials and testings delights our Lord![3]

LET THE DYING WITNESS

Let me ask you a question: Have you heard or read of the last words of atheists, agnostics, or other unbelievers? Did they express doubt or regret about their unbelief? By the scores I have read such accounts.

Atheists at Death

Voltaire, a famous French writer and unbeliever of the eighteenth century still studied today, said of Jesus: "Curse the wretch." He vowed, "In twenty years Christianity will be no more. My single hand shall destroy the edifice it took twelve apostles to rear." But his dying days were so filled with anguish that his nurse said, "For all the wealth in Europe I would not see another infidel die." His physician, a man named Trochim, reported that these were Voltaire's last words: "I am abandoned by God and man. I will give you half of what I am worth if you will give me six months' life. Then I shall go to hell; and you will go with me. O Christ. O Jesus Christ." Years after his death, Voltaire's house, which had been a factory for his anti-God propaganda, was purchased by the Geneva Bible Society to be used as a depot for Bibles.

Thomas Hobbes, a seventeenth-century English political philosopher whose thoughts have been used to deny God, came to a bleak end: "If I had the whole world, I would give it to live one day. I shall be glad to find a hole to creep out of the world. About to take a leap into the dark."

Edward Gibbon, author of the *Rise and Fall of the Roman Empire*, an epic history, died without Christ: "This day may be my last. I will agree that the immortality of the soul is at times a very comfortable doctrine. All this is now lost, finally, irrevocably lost. All is dark and doubtful."

Thomas Paine, a prominent author during the American Revolution, carried his rebellion against God throughout his life. But in his last hours he said, "I would give worlds, if I had them, that *Age of Reason* had not been published. O Lord, help me. Christ, help me. O God, what have I done to suffer so much? But there is no God. But if there should be, what will become of me hereafter? Stay with me, for God's sake. Send even a child to stay with me, for it is hell to be alone. If ever the devil had an agent, I have been that one."[4]

Now let me ask you this question: Can you name me one true follower of Jesus of Nazareth, the Messiah, who on the bed of death has said, "Jesus is a liar, and I regret ever following Him"?

Believers at Death

At death, who has ever been sorry for his belief in Jesus? I say no one, no, not one. Certainly not I. He is faithful and true. The only regrets that true followers of Christ may have are that they did not follow Him more closely, love Him more dearly, share Him more freely, and allow Him more control of their lives. But that precious decision to exchange their lives of sin for the Savior's precious atoning and forgiving life energizes and sustains Christians through the portals of death to the gates of heaven.

> *Can you name me one true follower of Jesus of Nazareth, the Messiah, who on the bed of death has said, "Jesus is a liar, and I regret ever following Him"?*

Regrets? If I had my life to live over, I would have trusted Christ sooner and sought to have the faith to recruit and train more Spirit-filled followers of Jesus to help fulfill the Great Commission. When Vonette and I were the only two staff of Campus Crusade for Christ, I prayed for one thousand staff. When we attained that level, I prayed for ten thousand staff. When we reached that number, I prayed for one million staff, and now (in early 2003) we know we have trained many millions of laypersons, and at least five hundred thousand staff faithfully serve Him today as members of our full-time and trained volunteer staff. Just as training is the key for athletes, astronauts, and soldiers, it is the absolute difference between nominal and meaningful Christianity. When you come to the end of the road or face your gravest test, that training in Christ stabilizes you as nothing else.

Jesus commanded, "Teach these new disciples to obey all the commands I have given you" (Matt. 28:20). Paul said, "You have heard me teach many things that have been confirmed by many reliable witnesses. Teach these great truths to trustworthy people who are able to pass them on to others" (2 Tim. 2:2). As believers, we should see that as our main business, always. Training is crucial. That's why I regret not believing God to train more workers. But never for a minute have I regretted giving my life to Christ. And the closer to death I come, the more thankful I am to have followed Him.

Martin Luther's last hour was filled with his memory of Scripture. He quoted John 3:16 and Psalm 68: "Our God is the God of whom cometh salvation. God is the Lord by whom we escape death." Three times he repeated, "Into thy hands I commend my spirit. Thou has redeemed me, O God of truth."

D. L. Moody with joy exclaimed, "I see earth receding, heaven is opening, God is calling me."

William Carey died in 1834 as "the father and founder of modern missions," and upon his deathbed, he said to a friend, "When I am gone, say nothing of me; speak about Dr. Carey's Savior." That expresses how I feel.

> *Never for a minute have I regretted giving my life to Christ.*

John Bunyan, author of *Pilgrim's Progress*, stated, "Weep not for me, but for yourselves. I go to the Father of our Lord Jesus Christ; Who will, no doubt, through the mediation of His Blessed Son, receive me, though a sinner: When I hope we shall ere long meet to sing the new song, and remain everlastingly happy, world without end, Amen."

George Washington, the victorious general of the American Revolutionary War, father of our country, and our first president, is my favorite person in all of history apart from biblical characters. He knew our Lord Jesus and always seemed to rise to the call of duty. During my first visit to Mount Vernon, his beautiful home on the Potomac, the guide took me to his bedroom and motioned to a chair at the end of his bed. Washington knelt there for an hour every morning and evening to read his Bible and pray. As he lay dying, he ordered that a tablet over the door of his tomb be inscribed with the promise of Jesus in John 11:25: "I am the resurrection and the life; he that believeth in Me, though he were dead, yet shall he live." Washington's last words were to his physician: "Doctor, I have been dying a long time; my breath cannot last long—but I am not afraid to die."

John Newton, the former slave trader who trusted Christ, became an abolitionist and preacher of the gospel. He was eighty-two when he told a visiting minister: "The Lord has a sovereign right to do what He pleases with His own. I trust we are His, in the best sense, by purchase, by conquest, and by our own willing consent. As sinners we have no rights, and as believing sinners we have no reason, to complain; for all our concerns are in the hand and care of our Best Friend, who has promised that all things shall work together for His glory and our final benefit. My trial is great, but I am supported, and have many causes for daily praise."[5]

Edward Payson, a prominent Congregationalist preacher, said, "The celestial City is in full view . . . I have been exulting yet almost trembling while I gaze on this excessive brightness, and wondering, with unutterable wonder, why God should stoop thus to shine upon a sinful worm like myself."

Karla Fay Tucker, as a drug-addicted prostitute, in 1983, murdered Jerry Dean and Deborah Thornton with a pick-ax. By 1998 she had been tried, found guilty, and ordered to be executed by the State of Texas. In the intervening years, she had received Jesus Christ as her personal Savior and Lord, followed Him in baptism and life, married a prison missionary, and spent years telling others of the truth that is in Jesus. Her last words according to the Associated Press were: "I am going to be face to face with Jesus now . . . I will see you all when you get there. I will wait for you."

The record of human witness is clear. Knowing God and having His perspective

> *Knowing God and having His perspective change everything about how we view death and dying.*

change everything about how we view death and dying. Can you imagine the great Creator-God and Savior with the power to have flung more than one hundred billion galaxies in space (most of them larger than our own Milky Way galaxy—the Savior who loves us so much He came to earth to die a horrible death on Calvary. Can you imagine this God letting anything happen to you or me that He will not lovingly work together for our good and His glory?[6] This is the magnificent risen Savior and Lord who walks with us through the valley of the shadow of death. We need not fear.

I join Paul in saying, "I am convinced that nothing can ever separate us from [God's] love. Death can't, and life can't. The angels can't, and the demons can't. Our fears for today, our worries about tomorrow, and even the powers of hell can't keep God's love away. Whether we are high above the sky or in the deepest ocean, nothing in all creation will ever be able to separate us from the love of God that is revealed in Christ Jesus our Lord" (Rom. 8:38–39).

"BLESSED ASSURANCE"

Blessed assurance, Jesus is mine!
O what a foretaste of glory divine!
Heir of salvation, purchase of God,
Born of His Spirit, washed in His blood.
This is my story, this is my song,
Praising my Savior all the day long;
This is my story, this is my song,
Praising my Savior all the day long.

—Fanny J. Crosby

THREE

"HOW ARE YOU DOING?"

That I may know Him and the power of His resurrection and the fellowship of His sufferings, being conformed to His death; in order that I may attain to the resurrection from the dead.

—THE APOSTLE PAUL (PHIL. 3:10–11 NASB)

Have you ever been walking along and your eyes meet someone walking toward you? You know what the person is about to say. It is, "How're you doing?" You want to be polite and honest. It can be hard to be both. I have a friend who long ago detected the insincerity of the question: "How are you doing?" He replies, "Do you really want to know? Do you have ten seconds or five minutes?" Only rarely does he receive a sympathetic, "Yes, friend, tell me how you are really feeling."

I have heard some people actually joke: "Don't ask him how he feels, or he'll tell you, and you'll be late for supper." We can chuckle because people can be long-winded, but if they have that much in their hearts to pour out, maybe the Lord is giving an opportunity for us to develop our listening skills. Some dear soul may need a listening ear as much as the wounded traveler needed the Good Samaritan's help. Surveys show that Americans spend 29.8 hours watching television each week—more than 4 hours per day—and yet the average amount of communication among family members is less than

30 minutes per day. That tells me lots of people need someone to listen.[1]

People often ask me how I am doing. If I believe the inquirer knows the Lord and is walking in His Spirit, I may say how my spirit really feels: "Rejoicing! I'm having a ball." This last season of my life on earth is the best in so many ways. I can write and read, listen to music, and focus on the Lord God as during no other time in my life; His agenda for my own little life is my only agenda. Every breath is a blessing and, some would say, a miracle. Vonette and I treasure our time together to grow in love and to help prepare for the brief time we may be physically separated one from another. God has been so gracious to give us what we consider an extended time together.

As we have seen, passing joyously through the valley of death involves special relationships with God, with loved ones, and with others whom we know well and some we do not know well. The overriding truth is to realize that the experience is a process; it will come to pass; and it will come to pass for His purposes.

PAIN IS A PROCESS

I like the acrostic developed by Dr. David Zimmerman of Atlanta in his "Grief Relief" Seminars.

Realize the Loss vs. Denying It

    Goal: To be able to say by faith: *"It happened."* Past tense. No "do over."

Experience the Pain vs. Protesting It

    Goal: To be able to admit by faith: *"I hurt."*

Let Time Help vs. Despairing

    Goal: To be able to say by faith: *"I need time."*

Increase Fellowship, Social Contact vs. Disconnecting in Isolation

    Goal: To be able to say by faith: *"I need you."*

Evaluate Loss vs. Lingering in Depression

    Goal: To be able to say by faith: *"I will work"* at learning from this.

Face the Future with Hope vs. Merely Resigning to Loss

Goal: To be able to say by faith: *"I will grow through this,"* not merely saying, "I will go through this."

We need to be able to say, "I needed help at the time, and I still do." Cry out to your friends and family and especially to God. Tears help heal. God keeps them in a bottle:

> You keep track of all my sorrows.
> You have collected all my tears in your bottle.
> You have recorded each one in your book. (Ps. 56:8)

What a tender friend is He!

Perhaps, as is many times the case, you may not appear on the outside to be particularly ill or suffering. My appearance changed little from the day I heard the first diagnosis of terminal illness. This can make it difficult for others to perceive your need. If it were a broken leg, it would be in a cast, and everyone could readily see the situation, the probable severity of the pain, and the likely prognosis and plan for recovery. Unfortunately, people often do not understand what they cannot see. If the source of pain is a broken heart, a terminal disease, a great loss, others may be slow to comprehend the suffering or understand the difficulties involved.

So be able to say, "We're just taking it one day at a time." By faith we speak these words, own the suffering, and slowly begin to engage others in our situation. Accept with gratitude whatever help others can give; do expect all you need from the Lord.

PEOPLE TO AVOID

There are some who, like the "friends" of Job or the Pharisees with whom Jesus had to deal, may be critical. They will analyze all your thoughts and behaviors, decide you have a multitude of sins to confess, and begin to itemize them for you. Run. When Peter evidenced a critical spirit, Jesus declared, "Get thee behind me, Satan" (Matt. 16:23 KJV). Of course, Peter was not literally Satan, but his words amounted to a satanic attack on the will of God in Jesus' life. You simply must avoid sources of accusation, condemnation, and discouragement as you heal. Do not fight them; avoid the discouragers, and let the Lord defend you.

A second group of unhelpful others includes those who are simply crude. A pastor friend in Florida told of a woman who would join the line of celebrants welcoming a decision-maker before the altar of the church. This lady greeted the joyfully tearful respondent with these words: "Don't worry, honey. You'll get over it." There are people like the one Bill Gaither once remembered: "She is so gloomy that when she enters the room, the lights go out." Flee these folks with the same speed that Joseph had in racing from the seductions of Potiphar's wife.

THE PARTNERSHIP IN SUFFERING

On the other hand, wonderful followers of Christ who have experienced pain and suffering can be truly gifted consolers. They have learned one of the important lessons about suffering: God allows it in our lives so that we will look to Him for comfort and strength, and then, when we meet others who are in the same difficulty, we can be of genuine support and encouragement to them—with compassion and conviction.[2]

Paul said that suffering is *not* to be borne alone. Trouble comes so that God can comfort us. Then with His holy scar tissue in our very souls, we can honestly confess understanding and empathy to others who fall into the same kinds of distress and sorrow. I have never experienced multiple sclerosis, for example, but I am prepared to share true and sensitive understanding with anyone who is suffering from pulmonary fibrosis—at a distinct level of empathy and authentic witness. Irony of ironies, I have that opportunity. Anne Wright, wife of my dear friend and devoted chief of staff Sid Wright, has been diagnosed with pulmonary fibrosis also. Yes, we can truly comfort one another because "we've been there," and we still are there.

C. S. Lewis contrasts the kind of help we need "when pain is to be borne." His words are in bold-faced type:[3]

"A little courage helps more than much knowledge." Encourage a person to take heart. This is not to offer false hope that there *definitely* will be complete, life-continuing miracles. Such assurances are ours to seek and God's to give. They are not for well-meaning but overzealous humans to announce. I believe the best thing to do is to offer the Christian's perspective that God is real, His promises are true, life is a brief and exciting journey, and heaven is our home. Jesus said, "I have told you all this so that you may have peace in me. Here on earth you will have many trials and sorrows. But take heart, because I have overcome the world" (John 16:33). Encouraging someone to stay vitally connected to Jesus is far superior to mere knowledge about death.

I am often asked the question, "How can I pray for you?" My answer always is: "Pray that I will never leave my first love." My number-one priority is my love relationship with our Lord Jesus, so it requires the most attention every hour of every day.

"A little human sympathy more than much courage." Deep in the dark night of the suffering soul comes a moment when nothing intellectual or psychological matters. It is the time of the touch, the tender touch, a hand held, a cheek kissed, a holy embrace that conveys more to the human spirit than anything from tongue or pen. Human compassion transmits what nothing else can do.

"The least tincture of the love of God more than all." Nothing exceeds God's love; its essence is His presence. God inhabits the praise of His people. He is a very present help in time of need. He draws very near to

> *Deep in the dark night of the suffering soul comes a moment when nothing intellectual or psychological matters.*

the suffering. How? By His Spirit indwelling the suffering person and by the witness of a follower of Christ, His presence comes with a card, a call, a gift, a visit. The visitor may ask simply, "Would you like to talk?" Sometimes, the mere listening presence of a friend is the greatest gift. We may invite our friend to walk, which is one of the most wonderful gifts of healing. We may ask, "Would you like for me to read something from the Bible? Do you have a favorite passage?" By all means, ask to pray for the suffering one. Singing and listening to Christian music always have meant much to me; in these days, they mean even more.

Although others may help some, we can expect much help from the Lord. Paul declared, "Last night an angel of the God to whom I belong and whom I serve stood beside me" (Acts 27:23). Innumerable are the accounts of believers who have the same testimony. God comes through in amazing ways to tend to the needs of His own. Count on Him.

Truly, loneliness can seem greater than suffering itself. Loneliness eats at the soul. But how does that loneliness arrive? It comes by self-pity. It comes when I take my eyes of faith off God and focus on my circumstances. It happens when I move from supernatural living—we see, for example, Peter walking on the water while gazing right at the Lord—to defeated living, as Peter turned his eyes to the storm and waves. This loneliness must be natural enough because it is described by such a giant of the faith as Paul. He knew he was in Christ and Christ was in him, but he still reached a point of physical isolation from others that he needed the eye of faith to see God beside him. Take heart, dear friend. You can say with Paul: "The Lord stood with me and gave me strength, that I might preach the Good News in all its fullness for all the Gentiles to hear. And he saved me from certain death" (2 Tim. 4:17).

The promises of God's Word sustain us in our suffering, and we know Jesus sympathizes and empathizes with us in our darkest hour: "That is why we have a great High Priest who has gone to heaven, Jesus the Son of God. Let us cling to him and never stop trusting him. This High Priest of ours understands our weaknesses, for he faced all of the same temptations we do, yet he did not sin. So let us come boldly to the throne of our gracious God. There we will receive his mercy, and we will find grace to help us when we need it" (Heb. 4:14–16).

God always gives hope. We have hope because we have Him. We have hope because He is with us. We have hope because He does not change. We have hope because His promises are true and He cannot deny His own Word:

> If we endure hardship, we will reign with him.
> If we deny him, he will deny us.
> If we are unfaithful,
>> He remains faithful,
>> for He cannot deny Himself. (2 Tim. 2:12–13)

He is ever faithful and gives us the song in the night to soothe our spirits and fresh joy each morning to lift our souls. What a marvelous Lord! Jesus said, "Come to me, all of you who are weary and carry heavy burdens, and I will give you rest" (Matt. 11:28).

Another precious promise for me—although it was given to the Israelites at a specific time for a specific purpose—holds within it the heart of God for us all in times of trial: "'For I know the plans I have for you,' says the LORD. 'They are plans for good and not for disaster, to give you a future and a hope'" (Jer. 29:11).

Wherever you are today on the journey of life, take courage. Don't give up. God has His eye on you, and He plans to meet you at the finish line. Press on, not in your own strength, but His, claiming His faithfulness.

SIGNS OF JOY

Sunsets. On several occasions Vonette and I enjoyed walking on the Pacific Ocean's beaches. How those sunsets help literally to measure our days. I love the beauty of them, whatever their scientific explanation. We visually absorb the artistry of God flowing from His palette of color. He never paints the same sunset twice, some crisp and clear, some turning clouds into prisms, creating a symphony of colors, and every one is a masterpiece.

Vonette and I also would walk the beautiful grounds of Arrowhead Springs at the closing of the day. After long journeys apart or at the end of hectic schedules, those walks were special. The sun descended beyond the rim of the Pacific Ocean, and there were those unique moments of twilight—neither daylight nor nightfall. The heat of the day was gone. The light coolness of the evening gently wafted through the San Bernardino Mountains. The Pacific sent a breeze. Together, these gifts of the Father refreshed us. The air seemed purer and easier to breathe. Lights came on in the San Bernardino Valley floor below; exactly when, we barely noticed. Then the last light of the sun blended into the first shadows of the night. We loved those walks. They were too few in number. Not with regret but with an honest heart, I came to see how much a couple need walks as much as they need talks.

Before our evening walk was over, the twilight passed, and suddenly two kinds of light kept total darkness at bay. The light in the city on the valley floor was artificial, but its twinkles and its flickers assured us of human life. We often wondered aloud and prayed over all those thousands of people in that valley. What was the condition of their souls? Did they know the Savior? How could we tell them? In what new and better ways? Oh, dear Lord, if we can look down upon such a beautiful sea of darkness and rejoice in electric lights below, how much more do You look down into the darkness of sin and celebrate the souls in whom the light of the Christ dwells? Did our Lord Jesus have to say more than this: "I am the light of the world"? If He uttered nothing more, it would have been enough for everyone to get the picture. Sin darkens the soul; Jesus brightens it up.

As darkness fell upon our walk, we would look up . . . oh, the wonder of His heavens at night. Where did those lights come from? Yes, from His very word. Remember, light was not already on its way and He merely allowed it to pass; no, He ordered light to show up, and light obeyed, and the world is blessed by that obedience.

The vast and deep, dark voids of a night sky make me wonder: How much more does God have in store? We are not to fear those dark holes; they are His handiwork too. And the stars would not be appreciated if the dark oceans of the universe were made light. For a sovereign God, designer of one unique creation, darkness has its mission as does light. Remember this in those long, dark nights of the soul when anguish would seem to engulf: you are one of the stars of God; He has given you light that this world needs to see. When the nights come, stand a faithful watch, a beacon for Him.

"O JESUS, I HAVE PROMISED"

O Jesus, I have promised to serve Thee to the end;
Be Thou forever near me, my Master and my Friend;
I shall not fear the battle if Thou art by my side,
Nor wander from the pathway if Thou wilt be my Guide.

O let me feel Thee near me, the world is ever near;
I see the sights that dazzle, the tempting sounds I hear:
My foes are ever near me, around me and within;
But, Jesus, draw Thou nearer, and shield my soul from sin.

—John E. Bode

FOUR

HE KNOWS THE WAY

This suffering is all part of what God has called you to.
Christ, who suffered for you, is your example. Follow in his steps.

—THE APOSTLE PETER (1 PETER 2:21)

*W*hen you travel in East Africa, especially Kenya, you are advised to seek out the *kiongozi*. This Swahili word identifies the local leader and guide who can take you safely through his particular territory, avoiding wild animals, literal pitfalls, poisonous snakes, and criminals. Of course, you can ignore the *kiongozi*; you can choose to be a foolish tourist, whip out a map, and try to make it on your own through the jungles. They will tell great tales of your bravado at your funeral.

It is always better to follow a leader who has been through what you are about to experience. Many people will give you their theories about why God allows suffering and pain and dying and death—most of them no wiser than the so-called fortune-tellers who prey on the weak with their "insights" and "readings" on television shows. Only the Lord Jesus is the Good Shepherd who goes ahead of His sheep and makes safe the trail. He promises that He is the way, the truth, and the life, and that He has gone to prepare a place for us. No one can come to the Father except through Him (John 14:6). Only the Lord Jesus has experienced life, death, and resurrection and reigns to intercede for us. Only Christ provides us hope beyond the grave. Only He sent the Holy Spirit to teach us of Him and to prepare each of us for the journey through death to heaven.

No matter what may happen to us, it is always right to look to Jesus and identify with Him and learn from His life. He is the Author and Finisher of our faith (Heb. 12:2). So, even in dying, I recommend that we identify with the Lord Jesus Christ and think of His example for us in how He died.

One day, my beloved Vonette asked me: "Why do you think you are suffering; why would God put you through this?"

Immediately, I sensed this reply in the Spirit: "I'm not suffering!" At least, it does not seem that way to me. Suffering is what our Lord endured. There is no comparison between what I'm going through and what

> *Suffering is what our Lord endured. There is no comparison between what I'm going through and what Christ went through.*

Christ went through. He was beaten beyond recognition; He spent six hours suffocating on the cross; He bore the sins of the world; He was cut off from God because of our sins for there was no other way for man to be redeemed. The agony of the trial that had been totally illegal. Then you can think about Peter being crucified upside down; Paul's persecution and his eventual beheading. All the disciples were persecuted and finally martyred, except John, who, after being burned in oil, then was exiled on an island by himself. Through the centuries there have been many martyrs. For their faith in Christ, millions more have spent many years in prisons infested with lice and rats, suffering torture and deprivation of all sorts.

"How can I say I am suffering when I am here in a bed of relative ease? I am surrounded by people who love me; suffering is a matter of perspective. It is not pleasant, humanly speaking. All disease comes from Satan, but God allows only so much—we can see those limits in the lives of Job, Joseph and others." Romans 5:3–5 says:

> "We can rejoice, too, when we run into problems and trials, for we know that they are good for us—they help us learn to endure. And endurance develops strength of character in us, and character strengthens our confident expectation of salvation. And this expectation will not disappoint us. For we know how dearly God loves us, because he has given us the Holy Spirit to fill our hearts with his love.

And think of Philippians 2:12–18:

> Dearest friends, you were always so careful to follow my instructions when I was with you. And now that I am away you must be even more careful to put into action God's saving work in your lives, obeying God with deep reverence and fear. For God is working in you, giving you the desire to obey him and the power to do what pleases him. In everything you do, stay away from complaining and arguing, so that no one can speak a word of blame against you. You are to live clean, innocent lives as children of God in a dark world full of crooked and perverse people. Let your lives shine brightly before them.
>
> Hold tightly to the word of life, so that when Christ returns, I will be proud that I did not lose the race and that my work was not useless. But even if my life is to be poured out like a drink offering to complete the sacrifice of your faithful service (that is, if I am to die for you), I will rejoice, and I want to share my joy with all of you. And you should be happy about this and rejoice with me.

I looked at Vonette and said: "We are most blessed; we are to look to God's grace, and oh, Father how great You are."

Vonette told a friend nearby: "Bill has been filled with such praise. What a man."

But, dear reader, please know I tell this so you can know for certain that God is faithful to His Word and He is present with you to help you through whatever stages of difficulty you may face. And my witness of His grace and faithfulness is only one of countless millions of hearts and minds who have experienced these glorious truths through the years.

1. He confronted, through prayer, the reality of dying. In the Garden of Gethsemane, the Lord Jesus faced the funeral music of His death. He was facing the bearing of our sin—He became sin who knew no sin that we might be made right in the eyes of God (2 Cor. 5:21). Yet in His humanity, He felt the same sense of impending doom and loss that we may feel. This helps me know that He knows how I feel. What a wonderful Savior!

"His sweat bacame like great drops of blood" (Luke 22:44 KJV). Those who have studied the details of Gethsemane say that medically this phenomenon is biologically possible for persons under unbearable stress. Understand how much Jesus did for us at Gethsemane. He dealt with the intellectual, psychological, and physical issues of dying. And how did He handle them? He took them to God in prayer. Should we do less? "I have given you an example to follow," He said. "Do as I have done to you" (John 13:15).

2. He desired fellowship. Again, as a man, He did not want to be alone. As the Son of God, He needed no one. But He wanted His friends around Him. And as the Son of man, He would have benefited from their prayers. His is a haunting question: "Then he returned and found the disciples asleep. 'Simon!' he said to Peter. 'Are you asleep? Couldn't you stay awake and watch with me even one hour?'" (Mark 14:37). Dear friends, this is one of the opportunities of being limited by dying and disease. By Jesus' example, we see it is perfectly normal to desire fellowship, even if it is restricted to telephone conversations and only rare visits. It is normal also to be a bit frustrated with those who do not "watch with [us] even one hour." Jesus had said that among the ways we live out our lives as unto Him is to visit the sick: "I assure you, when you refused to help the least of these my brothers and sisters, you were refusing to help me" (Matt. 25:45). So don't feel guilty for wanting to talk with others or for feeling frustrated when others don't make time for that fellowship. Jesus showed us by His example that fellowship is important.

3. *He made arrangements for His family.* While He was on the cross, Jesus saw His mother standing beside the apostle John, and He said to her: "'Woman, he is your son.' And he said to [John], 'She is your mother.' And from then on this disciple took her into his home" (John 19:26–27). In His dying hours, He cared for the bereavement His family would experience. He made sure someone trustworthy, loving, and faithful to the family would be there. We have the opportunity, the privilege, yes, and the duty to be there for others in their dying if we are invited. If you are not invited, make yourself available. If you are still not invited, do not go, but do pray faithfully. In complex societies of the developed world, dying is a bureaucratic experience. There are scores of details to handle, from funeral arrangements to death certificates, final tax returns to wills and courts and insurance companies. These are a burden to the family, and you will want to see that someone you trust handles those you cannot manage directly. In the developing world, where life is less complicated, there still remains the need to be sure the responsibilities you once carried for the family are handed to someone godly. It is a loving duty in your dying days.

4. *He faced the deadly details.* He refused the numbing gall He was offered because He was destined to experience *all* the pain and suffering anyone ever may experience (Matt. 27:34). He accepted no shortcuts in following the will of God for His life and death. The gall would have helped Him bear the pain of the cruel Roman cross. But He refused it so He could with integrity say to anyone dying: "My child, I do know how

you feel, though none other might know; I know and I care and I am going through this ordeal with you." As the writer of the book of Hebrews stated, "That is why we have a great High Priest who has gone to heaven, Jesus the Son of God. Let us cling to him and never stop trusting him. This High Priest of ours understands our weaknesses, for he faced all of the same temptations we do, yet he did not sin" (4:14–15). Yet Jesus on the cross was not insisting that His followers reject medicine. He chose to experience death fully. Crucifixion usually produced a fatal heart attack including asphyxiation.

During one of my trips to the hospital precipitated because I could hardly breathe, I told Vonette I was thanking God for giving me a glimpse of how our Lord experienced suffocation on the cross. I know that He knows what my dying will be like. Most of us will not die quickly. We are taken by the hand. Someone leads us to the hospital room, to the test, to the wheelchair, to the bath and bed. God allows this to let others share His love in kindness and caring, the very compassionate love of the Lord Jesus Himself.

At the same time, I do not insist that others take Christ's example in refusing the gall as a reason not to accept medical treatments. However, I truly do not wish to be drugged just to extend my life.

5. He expressed His physical, intellectual, and emotional feelings. His emotions were raging in being alone, separated from eternal fellowship with the Father. "Jesus called out with a loud voice, 'Eloi, Eloi, lama sabachthani?' which means, 'My God, my God, why have you forsaken me?'" (Mark 15:34). He hurt in His body, and He said so: "I am thirsty" (John 19:28). He was miserable as He bought mercy and grace for us with His very life. See the humanity of this, and give yourself permission to feel the loneliness, isolation, pain, and sense of loss that you may be experiencing. Yet never forget the purposeful example of Jesus in expressing His feelings to others and to God the Father. God is our best refuge for our hurts and frustrations as life ebbs from our bodies: "So let us come boldly to the throne of our gracious God. There we will receive his mercy, and we will find grace to help us when we need it" (Heb. 4:16).

By His example He freed us from trying to pretend that dying does not hurt; of course, it does. For some it is physical pain that hurts most; for others, it is the loneliness; for still others there is a mental and intellectual agony. Express the feelings to the Father who loves you and is there with you. And gain God's perspective: "For our present troubles are quite small and won't last very long. Yet they produce for us an

> *By His example He freed us from trying to pretend that dying does not hurt; of course, it does.*

immeasurably great glory that will last forever! So we don't look at the troubles we can see right now; rather, we look forward to what we have not yet seen. For the troubles we see will soon be over, but the joys to come will last forever" (2 Cor. 4:17–18).

6. Jesus pointed us to the Scriptures. He was quoting Scripture as He was dying (Matt. 27:46 refers to Ps. 22:1). Have you hidden the Word of God in your heart against that day of your greatest test? What a witness to your family, children, grandchildren, neighbors, and friends when they see that, like Jesus, your dying words include the holy Scriptures. Be regular but not ritualistic about this; the power is in developing your knowledge of God, not in any formula. As you are daily reading the Word of God, the Spirit of God will pray for you, comfort you, and bring to your mind the Scriptures you need. Jesus reassured us: "When the Father sends the Counselor as my representative—and by the Counselor I mean the Holy Spirit—he will teach you everything and will remind you of everything I myself have told you" (John 14:26).

7. *He witnessed while dying.* He was on a mission to redeem mankind. He never ducked that duty or wavered from it. To the dying thief on a nearby cross, Jesus declared, "I assure you, today you will be with me in paradise" (Luke 23:43). Dr. Billy Graham has said this "deathbed confession" of the thief is an example that occurs only once in the ministry of Jesus—once that no man should fear and only once that no man should presume upon God. Dying gives us many opportunities to witness for Christ.

A dear friend, whom I will call Beth, was admitted to a Florida hospital with brain wave problems, but because the neurology section of the hospital was full, she was placed for one night only in a cardiac care unit. The elderly woman in the adjoining bed, who happened to be Jewish, was in intense pain and expressed great fear about dying. Around 3:00 A.M., Beth heard the woman groaning and crying out: "I'm dying. I'm dying." Although Beth could not walk, she got down from her own bed and crawled across the room on hands and knees to go to the dying woman's bedside. There she bent over the elderly woman's body and kindly, urgently, and clearly witnessed to her of the love of Yeshua, the Savior of all, the Messiah. Beth gave her the good news and prayed with her the simple prayer, asking God for salvation through faith in our Lord Jesus Christ. Beth asked the dying woman to squeeze her hand if she understood and if she had prayed the suggested prayer. The woman squeezed Beth's hand positively, and "her countenance changed completely," Beth recalled. Within minutes she was rushed away and did not return.

Later, Beth learned the woman had died. But her destination was heaven, and her destiny changed eternally because a faithful Christian witnessed through her own pain. That is what Jesus did on the cross. Ironically, before her hospitalization occurred, Beth had been praying especially for Jewish people to know Jesus. Are you ready to witness? For whom are you praying?

8. He settled accounts for eternity. "When Jesus had tasted it, he said, 'It is finished!' Then he bowed his head and gave up his spirit" (John 19:30). Jesus was able to say He fulfilled His mission on this planet. His objective, though physical in form, was a spiritual mission in its essence. Each human has a spirit. That is what separates human beings from animals and insects, fish and fowl. In demonstrating His own faith while dying, Jesus—while fully in control of His faculties—committed His Spirit unto God the Father. May I ask you: Have you done that? You can today.

Yes, even as you may lie dying, you can make the final transaction to reaffirm and reconfirm your faith in Christ. Make it a bold and wonderful declaration of your trust—your utter and complete dependence on God for your salvation.[1]

I am reminded of a little girl and her father who went hiking in the Smoky Mountains. They came upon a narrow river, and at four years old, she was fearful of the river's current. She turned and ran back. "Come to me," her dad said.

She ran to his arms, saying, "Can you take me, Daddy?"

"Sure, let's go," her father said as he picked her up and waded easily across the stream.

"Look at the waves," the child said, describing the small ripples of water. "I see a fish," she said gleefully. She was now calm. Fear had disappeared as she trusted her father.

Even so, in death, we can count on our heavenly Father to carry us across the cold waters of death, and we can rest in His arms and enjoy the view.

While our Lord Jesus modeled for us important steps to take in facing death and enduring suffering, He also gave His followers what may be His most tender promise: "And be sure of this: I am with you always, even to the end of the age" (Matt. 28:20).

"I'd Rather Have Jesus"

I'd rather have Jesus than silver or gold,
I'd rather be His than have riches untold;
I'd rather have Jesus than houses or lands,
I'd rather be led by His nail-pierced hand.
Than to be the king of a vast domain or be held in sin's dread sway;
I'd rather have Jesus than anything this world affords today.

—Rhea F. Miller

PAIN AND GRACE

Religious faith is not a storm cellar to which men and women can flee for refuge from the storms of life. It is, instead, an inner spiritual strength which enables them to face those storms with hope and serenity.

—SAM ERVIN, CHRISTIAN AND U.S. SENATOR, 1983

In the motion picture *Shadowlands*, a professor watches his wife dying of cancer at their home. She seems to be suffering unmercifully slowly but with courage beyond human expression. Their eyes meet, and it seems that more understanding of all humanity's condition passes between them in that moment than in all the professor's lectures to thousands of students throughout his career.

Her name is Joy, and the irony of Joy lying amid pain underlies the entire experience. She manages a smile, not a grimace, but a pure smile, and he knows what her heart is communicating. It is a knowing beyond knowing, explaining, or describing. He knows her so well that he can tell how she is feeling without asking the question or analyzing her reply. She knows what he is thinking without his speaking, and she chooses to respond in a way that is in his best interest, not hers. He attends to practical details—water, medicine, a walk, a hug, the bedsheets, the food, and the slow but not imperceptible change of her body, their home, and their lives. Time and disease are overcoming physical desire and expression. But he feels strangely uncomfortable with all the practicalities; rather, he wants, if he could, to change places with her or to somehow place his strength inside hers, to help her bear the ever-burdening pain.

Without words they seem to shout their love for each other. Without written and formal declaration, they seem to pronounce their resolve to take in the life that is in every moment, to savor its taste, to share its joyful and mournful reality and, soon enough, to swallow its bittersweet portion. The motion picture was based on the true story of the wife of C. S. Lewis, the gifted writer and agnostic who became one of history's most effective Christian apologists.

I know something of this valley of the shadow of death, too. As a leader of visitation at the First Presbyterian Church of Hollywood, California, while still in my late twenties, I had a remarkable experience of the "peace that passes all understanding" surrounding the time of life's end. On the visitation list that evening were an older couple in their eighties. They were living in a small trailer located on a parking lot in downtown Hollywood. He had been a very successful businessman, and they had known considerable wealth, but because of massive medical expenses over a period of years, they were now reduced to poverty. At the very moment I entered their little trailer home, what I saw became etched in my memory for all time.

A PURE WITNESS

The couple sat side by side. He held her hand with his left hand and, from time to time, patted her hand with his right to communicate confident assurance. Money was no issue. Their love was. Her eyes twinkled at him, and he was totally devoted to her care. They spoke often of the Lord and pointed me to Scriptures. They made it clear that she was ready to meet their Lord, and he was going to miss her but would join her soon enough. They spoke of heaven as if it were home. They spoke of seeing the Lord Jesus more certainly than they were seeing me. We prayed together, and I felt as if I had been in the presence of angels.

I walked away from their little abode with a conviction: they knew the Lord Jesus. They were not afraid of death. They were completing their journey home. Heaven awaited. The witness of their lives was so compelling, I was never the same. The pure, loving witness of that dear couple convincingly defeated whatever theological debate I have ever confronted. It was one of the most meaningful, moving experiences of my life. I had hoped to be a blessing to them. Instead they were a profound blessing to me.

And I say with them: God knows we are going home. He is with us. The journey is not much longer. The arrival will be glorious. My beloved Vonette has been with me every step of the way. We have rejoiced in what God has done and is doing through our fifty-four years together. As a result, we cannot be anything but humbly grateful.

THE INTRUDER

But the pain of dying enters unannounced. The longer it lingers, the more it presses the questions: How will you handle it? Must you handle it? Its presence is like a "For Sale" sign placed in your yard. A newcomer—death—is soon to occupy your old house, the one you have lived in all these years, in joy and sadness, in triumph and loss, alone and with wonderful loved ones. You are going to move out, but you must keep residing until the contract is signed and all of the arrangements are made. While you abide, pain leers in the windows, but as you turn on the light of God's Word, it slinks away.

Pain and I have met a few times. Pain visited in common and small ways. But after nearly eighty-two years of living, I now know dying pain is different from any other. It is riveting, demanding, disrespectful, discourteous, and unkind—yet it is truly a friend to faith. It presses you to your core beliefs. It gives no quarter, expects everything, and takes all it can as long as it can. Nevertheless, death is a defeated foe, conquered by Jesus of Nazareth, our great Creator-God and Savior. And death must submit to His commands. As a result, the coming of death merely creates opportunities for eternal life to flood my living. This is the paradox: death produces life as life gives way to death.

Paul wrote, "Through suffering, these bodies of ours constantly share in the death of Jesus so that the life of Jesus may also be seen in our bodies. Yes, we live under constant danger of death because we serve Jesus, so that the life of Jesus will be obvious in our dying bodies" (2 Cor. 4:10–11). God the Father has allowed my body to be struck in the physical sense, but the striking has only set off a spiritual vibration, and the tone and pitch of it are of heaven in my soul.

Suffering can be liberating in its confinement. Limited by medical realities and doctor's orders, I am applying in a new way certain disciplines of living learned long ago. I allow no rivals for the God-sent priorities in my life, and this generates new joys and energy. Now, with plainly perceivable reason, I can say no to anything and everything that is not on the very top of God's agenda for my life. This is one of the joys of dying: constant dialogue with the Savior of my soul to be sure I am finishing the course He intended for me, not someone else, not for some other purpose, only His will and His way and His timing. I find another paradox: the more quantity of life that dying steals, the greater quality of life it leaves for my enjoyment. I have learned whatever state I am in to be content, said Paul, and this same contentment is available in dying—as it is in living—to all followers of Jesus (Phil. 3:11 NIV).

VANITY, GOOD-BYE

The presence of dying pain forces me to open myself up to our Savior God at the expense of my withering physical self. Vanity, especially, must leave the rooms of my life. It is far too time-consuming and utterly void of eternal value, but dying has helped to dispel it like no decision of the will ever could. This simply is another phase of obedience in following Jesus. "He must increase, but I must decrease," John the Baptist said (John

3:30 NASB). It cost John his life, but Jesus emerged for the world as predicted by the forerunner.

All this may seem common to some and preposterous to others. I witnessed its reality in the dying of my saintly mother and of my father and of my sister and brothers and so many others in the great family of faith I have known. But up close and personal, this dying, this joyous germ, had not afflicted me until I entered my seventies. I was too busy to honor pain, to make room for disease, to settle for sickness. I was consumed with helping to fulfill the Great Commission in my generation and compelled to push through the ordinary illnesses. I wanted to see results, not feel the pangs of disease, much less dying. Death in a plane crash? No problem, I had always felt. A life-ending heart attack? That would not be so bad, I had usually concluded. But slow and choking death, doctors told me, would be another matter.

My mind had the knowledge of holy Scriptures on the subject. Intellectually, I knew God would see me through such days when they came. "I know whom I have believed and am persuaded that He is able to keep what I have committed to Him until that Day," the apostle Paul said plainly (2 Tim. 1:12 NKJV). We know the same Lord Jesus, Paul and I, and Paul—next to our Lord Jesus—has been my mentor most of my life. So I took calm assurance that Jesus would see me through. Still this particular battle, the struggle inside the body and in the spirit, I could not fully anticipate. As a spiritual issue, I thought I was ready for it. It would be the same equation as the other tests and trials and tribulations of life: "No temptation has overtaken you except such as is common to man; but God is faithful, who will not allow you to be tempted beyond what you are able, but with the temptation will also make the way of escape; that you may be able to bear it" (1 Cor. 10:13 NKJV).

By faith Vonette and I had claimed such promises for sustenance in many an hour. And they had proven true countless times in the lives God has allowed Vonette and me to live.

The journey we are on is not necessarily a map or to-do list for others. Dying pain touches each in its own way. The victories Vonette and I have known may not be the same as those victories you can experience.

But our Savior God, the Lord Jesus, has personally promised He will be stronger in us by His Spirit as we grow weaker in our flesh. Paul declared, "Each time he said, 'My gracious favor is all you need. My power works best in your weakness.' So now I am glad to boast about my weaknesses, so that the power of Christ may work through me" (2 Cor. 12:9).

Jesus interrupted Paul's pain-filled days with that promise. It is a joyful discovery to be reading a red-lettered edition of the Bible, in which all the type is black, and the pages can seem oppressively gray. But the words of Jesus appear in red ink, and suddenly, we turn to that precious passage in 2 Corinthians 12:9 (NKJV): "My grace is sufficient for you, for My strength is made perfect in weakness."

What a powerful promise from the most powerful Person! The unmerited sustaining grace of Jesus of Nazareth has been keeping me all these years, and He is yet applying it as a precious ointment to my soul in these dying days. This is the God who, I say from a bed of affliction, still raises the dead and still gives strength for the living and grace for the dying. With Paul I say, "Since I know it is all for Christ's good, I am quite content with my weaknesses and with insults, hardships, persecutions, and calamities. For when I am weak, then I am strong" (2 Cor. 12:10).

SUFFICIENCY IN SUFFERING

Listen again to the words of Jesus in Paul's time of extreme distress, a time of physical, mental, and spiritual duress:

> My grace (My favor and loving-kindness and mercy) is enough for you [sufficient against any danger and enables you to bear the trouble manfully]; for My strength and power are made perfect (fulfilled and completed) and show themselves most effective in [your] weakness. Therefore, I will all the more gladly glory in my weaknesses and infirmities, that the strength and power of Christ (the Messiah) may rest (yes, may pitch a tent over and dwell) upon me! (2 Cor. 12:9 AMPLIFIED)

Most believers know the definition of the *grace* of God as the "unmerited favor" of God. We can never earn it. Yet Paul wrote, "My God shall supply all your need according to His riches in glory by Christ Jesus" (Phil. 4:19 NKJV). From that promise someone developed an acrostic to explain grace as

God's

Riches

At

Christ's

Expense

That wonderfully describes the grace of God. "So let us come boldly to the throne of our gracious God. There we will receive his mercy, and we will find grace to help us when we need it" (Heb. 4:16). Someone must pay the bill for the essentials of time and eternity, and the Lord God through Christ always steps to the pay window to provide enough to settle our account. There is no way to manufacture grace or manipulate it. But we can ask for it, we can expect it, and we can receive it.

The most amazing thing about grace to the suffering heart and soul is its utter sufficiency. Jesus said, "My grace is sufficient for you." Do you believe that? I have experienced it to be so.

He promised that sufficiency to Paul who battled "a thorn in the flesh" that tossed him around over an extended period of time. The thorn was rude and demanding the way dying pain is. It interrupts your day and reschedules your life. It gruffly takes you along a brambled path. Paul begged God to remove the thorn of suffering. But the Lord ever said, "My grace is sufficient."

On the thorny path, past the shadows, through the valley, up the mountain, down the ravine, the sufficiency of His grace sustains us. What does that mean? Paul quoted Jesus as using the word, in Greek, *arketos*, and it appears only twice in the New Testament. It means more than merely "enough." As with many words of that language, it swirls with full and rich aspects of meaning, all comforting, all satisfying. If you stand in the heat of summer on a Greek island, you feel breezes coming from all different directions, literally from the four winds, and every single one refreshes. The sufficiency of God's grace is like that. It is just the right amount of just the right quality arriving as if from nowhere at just the right time.

Imagine a master chef directing a helper to pour portions of an oil into a cooking pan. "Enough," the chef commands. No more, no less. The chef says it is now prepared for the heat. Sometimes grace may be lavishly poured out, and other times it may be only a pinch, a smidgen, but always it is just right, enough, satisfying, making content for the occasion. As a young businessman in Hollywood, California, in my B.C. (before Christ) days, I developed a line of fine confections known as Bright's Epicurean Delights. The appeal of the products lay in their taste being the exactly right balance of ingredients for the customer. Only the chef and creator of these treats knew the right recipe. So it is with our lives. We need the supernatural knowledge and judgment of our great Creator-God to mix into our lives the precise amount of grace sufficient for the hour we are in. Only He can do it, but He definitely knows what we need! (Too often, we may find ourselves trying to tell God what we need. He knows! He knows! By way of comparison, I do not recall a single one of Bright's Epicurean Delights ever rising up in protest to tell me what to do, when to do it, or how much of anything to add to its existence. It rested in the judgment of its maker.)

The sufficiency of the grace of God amounts to portions of His love delivered on time and in the best way. It comes in a manner that is kind and comforting, easy to receive, not frightening but assuring. Its form is custom-designed for each of us, as God makes fruit of different forms fit for different seasons and different palates. The grace of God is the one thing we cannot do without in this life or in the life to come; it has no substitutes, artificial, temporary, or otherwise. Its quality exceeds minimum requirements, and it stirs all our senses in the most kind ways. Its touch feels ideal, its sound caresses the soul, its fragrance relaxes the nerves, its taste refreshes and satisfies, and its sight is that of the dearest relative or friend arriving in the doorway at the loneliest moment of our being. Grace, grace, God's grace, nothing like it, flowing straight from the heart of our wonderful Savior and Lord to the wounds of our lives. In sum, think of the *sufficiency* of grace being

Good—in every way it is a quality we welcome.

Real—it is present, perceivable, and precious.

Essential—it is the one thing we need.

Ample—it is always the right amount.

Timely—it arrives in season, in emergency, at the exact moment it must.

Hear Him say it again to you: "My grace is sufficient for all your needs." Hallelujah, what a Savior!

To illustrate, let me tell you of a friend of many years who calls me once a week. I am sure there are many others who would like to call, and I deeply thank them for their prayers. But I have known this man so long, it is so very easy to be totally transparent with him. I can depend on his call. I can tell him my latest struggles. While finishing this manuscript, for example, I experienced having to be bathed in bed for the first time. The world in which I can walk is virtually gone. But my friend encourages and rejoices with me, and I with him. He helps me stay focused on rejoicing in the Lord. I have always sought to learn something from everyone, and even in these hours, I am learning—on the receiving end—the great value of a personal telephone call. I have often sought to minister to others by prayer on the telephone. Now God is blessing me on a return channel!

> *I have always sought to learn something from everyone, and even in these hours, I am learning.*

"In the Garden"

I come to the garden alone, while the dew is still on the roses;
And the voice I hear, falling on my ear, the Son of God discloses.
And He walks with me, and He talks with me,
And He tells me I am His own;
And the joy we share as we tarry there,
None other has ever known.

—C. Austin Miles

DISCIPLINES OF ETERNAL LIFE

I am but a foreigner here on earth;
I need the guidance of your commands.
Don't hide them from me!

—Ps. 119:19

If we walked together on Fifth Avenue in New York City, we would see a powerful contrast between two buildings. In the entrance of the RCA building is a statue of Atlas, a perfectly formed man, straining with all his muscles as he tries to hold the world on his shoulders. Indeed, that is one way to live, each of us trying to carry the weight of the world. But if we simply walk across the street to Saint Patrick's Cathedral, we would find a better way. Behind the altar in that great sanctuary is a simple shrine of the boy Jesus, about eight or nine, holding the world in one hand.

Which is it for you? God can handle whatever comes into our lives if we let Him. Someone asked, "Is God a micromanager?" The question implies that God is too busy to bother with the little things in our lives, and that it is somehow distasteful to believe in a God who might be such a busybody that He would meddle in our lives.

My response is this: not the devil, not the genius, but God is in the details. He will manage whatever we ask Him to. He does not intrude except where He is invited. But He very much cares about little things in our lives. As the great Creator-God, He saw to "every living thing." As the God-man and Savior, Jesus of Nazareth took care of turning water into wine and feeding five thousand with five loaves and two fish. He personally tended to each person brought to Him. "Give all your worries and cares to God, for he cares about what happens to you" (1 Peter 5:7).

For me and my house, I can say that He has managed detail upon detail. Even as I am here in the hospital writing this book, the nurse was unable after many attempts to draw a blood sample. We stopped the procedure. Vonette and I immediately prayed and asked God to intervene and undertake. We prayed for the nurse as she wielded the needle and for my body to yield the necessary blood. Only seconds after our "amen," the nurse announced, "There!"

Is that mere coincidence? If we are living in vital union with the Lord, as He suggests we do in John 15, living as the branches of the Vine, I believe everything we do by faith, trusting in His promises, is directed by the Spirit of God for His glory and our good. I wish I had a dollar for the thousands upon thousands of times God has heard and answered my prayers for what seemed like little things—from parking spaces to passports to precious moments and priceless memories. On countless occasions we have prayed for the salvation of souls, safety for travelers, and specific amounts of money—and received direct, specific answers. If I could add up all those answered prayers, they would make a sizable praise offering to Him for establishing discipleship and evangelistic training centers around the globe. Yes, God is in the details, and so must we be there to welcome Him to our lives.

On one occasion, Vonette had lost her contact lens. There was not even the slightest clue where to look for it. After a fruitless effort of more than an hour trying to find it, I suggested to our son Zac, who had joined me in the search, that we stop and pray: "God knows where it is. Why don't we stop searching and ask Him?" The moment we ended our prayer, we opened our eyes, and there at my feet, glistening in the morning sun, was Vonette's contact lens. Yes, God is interested in details.

THE BASICS

When Vince Lombardi was the very successful head coach of the Green Bay Packers professional football team, someone asked what his secrets to success were. He explained that at his first meeting with a team, each year he would hold up an oblong leather object and say, "This is a football." He then said success would come as the men committed to "block and tackle." Basics, ever the basics.

In any endeavor the basics may sometimes seem boring, but practicing them is the key to victory. Musicians practice the same scales. Athletes run the same laps. How much more important it is for a follower of Jesus to go to the heavenly Father and demonstrate repeated obedience.

> *Let me urge you: do not be satisfied with superficial Christianity.*

Let me urge you: do not be satisfied with superficial Christianity, but really make sure you are experiencing basic salvation through biblical faith and practice. When it comes to the end of earth's journey, nothing is going to satisfy but the basics.

Prayer

That is why for most of my Christian life I have started each day on my knees (except for these last months I have remained in bed). My prayer is, "Lord, I want to be a suit of clothes for You today. I invite You to move around in my body as Your temple. I ask You to think with my mind, love with my heart, speak with my lips, and continue to seek and save the lost through me. Supervise and control my attitudes, my motives, my desires, my words, my actions in order to bring maximum glory to Yourself."

Continually aware of the sinfulness of my old nature, the old Bill Bright and how prone I would be to disobey God if my old nature should be victorious over my new nature (Rom. 8:7–8; Gal. 5:16–17), I have prayed on thousands of occasions: "Holy Father, if there is a chance that I will ever do anything to dishonor You or be unfaithful to my beloved Vonette, please take my life before it can happen."

Meditation

The psalmist wrote, "I lie awake thinking of you, meditating on you through the night" (Ps. 63:6), and "I will study your commandments and reflect on your ways" (Ps. 119:15). I have memorized many verses of Scripture, but in addition I have made it a point to focus on the attributes of God and consciously meditate on them once or more each day:

- Because God is a personal Spirit, I will seek intimate fellowship with Him.

- Because God is all-powerful, He can help me with anything.

- Because God is ever present, He is always with me.

- Because God knows everything, I will go to Him with all my questions and concerns.

- Because God is sovereign, I will joyfully submit to His will.

- Because God is holy, I will devote myself to Him in purity, worship, and service.

- Because God is absolute truth, I will believe what He says and live accordingly.

- Because God is righteous, I will live by His standards.

- Because God is just, He will always treat me fairly.

- Because God is love, He is unconditionally committed to my well-being.

- Because God is merciful, He forgives me of my sins when I sincerely confess them.

- Because God is faithful, I will trust Him to always keep His promises.

- Because God never changes, my future is secure and eternal.

This spiritual discipline has been such a blessing to me that I encourage every believer, especially anyone who is sick and needy, to make this your practice as well.

The Word of God

If I could be with you today as a life coach, I would hold up the Bible and say, "This is the book of Jesus. Love Him, trust His promises, and obey His commands recorded in this inspired Holy Book."

One day as I was reading the books of 1 and 2 Kings, I realized vividly how important the temple is to God and how focused followers of the one, true God were upon the Ten Commandments, which were central in the temple. The apostle Paul told us our bodies are the temples of the Holy Spirit. So I decided the Ten Commandments should be central to my temple. Before I read the Scripture each morning and each evening, I review and meditate on the following:

1. I am the Lord your God; do not worship any other gods besides Me.

2. Do not make idols of any kind.

3. Do not misuse the name of the Lord your God.

4. Remember to observe the Sabbath day by keeping it holy.

5. Honor your father and mother.

6. Do not murder.

7. Do not commit adultery.

8. Do not steal.

9. Do not testify falsely against your neighbor.

10. Do not covet.

Then I quote the Golden Rule: "Do to others as you would have them do to you" (Luke 6:31 NIV).

Next I frequently quote aloud our Lord's Great Command: "'Love the Lord your God with all your heart, all your soul, all your strength, and all your mind.' And, 'Love your neighbor as yourself'" (Luke 10:27), and "the love passage" of 1 Corinthians 13:4–13:

> Love is patient and kind. Love is not jealous or boastful or proud or rude. Love does not demand its own way. Love is not irritable, and it keeps no record of when it has been wronged. It is never glad about injustice but rejoices whenever the truth wins out. Love never gives up, never loses faith, is always hopeful, and endures through every circumstance. Love will last forever, but prophecy and speaking in unknown languages and special knowledge will all disappear. Now we know only a little, and even the gift of prophecy reveals little! But when the end comes, these special gifts will all disappear. It's like this: When I was a child, I spoke and thought and reasoned as a child does. But when I grew up, I put away childish things. Now we see things imperfectly as in a poor mirror, but then we will see everything with perfect clarity. All that I know now is partial and incomplete, but then I will know everything completely, just as God knows me now. There are three things that will endure— faith, hope, and love—and the greatest of these is love.

ARMOR AND POWER

As I prayerfully and carefully do these things, I am conscious that I am, in effect, putting on the armor of God cited by Paul in Ephesians 6:13–18:

Use every piece of God's armor to . . . stand your ground, putting on the sturdy belt of truth and the body armor of God's righteousness. For shoes, put on the peace that comes from the Good News, so that you will be fully prepared. In every battle you will need faith as your shield to stop the fiery arrows aimed at you by Satan. Put on salvation as your helmet, and take the sword of the Spirit, which is the word of God. Pray at all times and on every occasion in the power of the Holy Spirit. Stay alert and be persistent in your prayers for all Christians everywhere.

Then I deliberately ask our Lord to continue to cleanse me of all my sins of omission and commission with His precious blood shed on the cross for my sins. I invite the Holy Spirit to continually fill me, control and empower me, that I may please, honor, and glorify God.

I take literally our Lord's command to seek first His kingdom and His righteousness (Matt. 6:33). So before I eat breakfast or do anything else, I read His Word, the Bible, and pray to be sure my mind and spirit are nourished. I acknowledge afresh that I am His slave, fully surrendered to do His will for the day.

Are these legalistic acts of a dead ritual, or are they vital repetition? I believe God uses the Word we have hidden in our hearts. I believe when He promises blessings and prosperity as we "meditate" day and night on His Word, He is saying to repeatedly train ourselves, to fortify our minds with His Word. Therefore, it is a matter of obedience: "Study this Book of the Law continually. Meditate on it day and night so you may be sure to obey all that is written in it. Only then will you succeed" (Josh. 1:8).

REWARDS OF REPETITION

Truly it has been said, the Word of God will keep you from sin, or sin will keep you from His Word. We are admonished: "Be diligent to present yourself approved to God as a workman who does not need to be ashamed, accurately handling the word of truth" (2 Tim. 2:15 NASB).

So I am constantly working to do five things with the Word of God:

1. Hear.

2. Read.

3. Study.

4. Memorize.

5. Meditate.

And I give this testimony: daily reading His Word and memorizing it have sustained me when nothing else could. When Scriptures come to mind in conversations with others, I quote them. When I am explaining decisions, I cite my sources in the Word of God, the Holy Bible. It is glorious food for the brain as well as the soul.

One of the joys of these past two years has been the opportunity to praise our Lord in the quiet, precious ways I always enjoyed but was often interrupted from while traveling and ministering day and night around the world. I commend to every believer the listening of praise tapes. Allowing ourselves to praise Him, to join in hymns and spiritual songs, truly brings melody to the heart and very practically relieves stress, refocuses the mind on things eternal, and reminds us of His marvelous attributes (Eph. 5:19; Col. 3:16).

For example, I love the message of Andrae Crouch's song:

> I thank God for the mountains,
> And I thank Him for the valleys;
> I thank Him for the storms He brought me through;
> For if I'd never had a problem,
> I wouldn't know that He could solve them
> I'd never know what faith in God could do.[1]

AUTHORITY OF THE BIBLE

Some may deride my life as that of "another Bible-thumper." I do not thump the Bible; I rather let it thump me. It is my source of discipline, encouragement, strength, joy, praise, and thanksgiving, and my attitudes about life—be they good, bad, and indifferent. Everyone can have his own opinion about the Bible, but I must ask, Whose word do you base your life upon? The fables of poets, the one-liners on television, the lyrics of intoxicated, pot-smoking singers, the anti-God themes of Hollywood movies, the God-mocking writers of anti-Christian publishers?

Do you think we can depend upon the Bible in hard times? I do. I believe the Bible to be the holy, inspired Word of God because it reliably claims to be. The phrase "Thus says the Lord" appears more than two thousand times, and the biblical writers noted, "All Scripture is inspired by God and is useful to teach us what is true and to make us realize what is wrong in our lives. It straightens us out and teaches us to do what is right" (2 Tim. 3:16), and "No prophecy was ever made by an act of human will, but men moved by the Holy Spirit spoke from God" (2 Peter 1:21 NASB).

I believe the Bible is the Word of God because it is the book of Jesus. The Old Testament has more than three hundred prophecies concerning the promised Messiah, which were fulfilled by Jesus. He is recorded as quoting the five books of Moses, and those of Daniel, Isaiah, Jeremiah, the Psalms, and Jonah. He lived the Gospels, is the reason for and theme of the Acts of the Apostles, predicted the Epistles (John 16:13–15), and personally gave the Revelation. In fact, the New Testament has more than one thousand references to the Old Testament, including 1 Corinthians 10:11, which (referring to the history of the Israelites) declares, "All these events happened to them as examples for us. They were written down to warn us, who live at the time when this age is drawing to a close."

Jesus said to an audience that had only the Old Testament: "You search the Scriptures because you think that in them you have eternal life; it is these that testify about Me" (John 5:39 NASB).

For many years I have taught that the Holy Spirit is to the believer as one wing of an airplane, and the Word of God represents the other wing. Our Lord Jesus Christ is the pilot. If we do not rely on the Holy Spirit to guide us and also saturate ourselves with God's truth—His holy, inspired, inerrant truth—then our holy life will not fly. We must always invite Jesus to be the navigator of our plans, desires, wills, and emotions, for He is the way, the truth, and the life. We need never doubt what is right or wrong; we can look to God's Word. We have in Jesus Christ a perfect example of how to put God's truth into practice. And we have the power of the Holy Spirit to enable us to live the truth (Zech. 4:6).

> *We must always invite Jesus to be the navigator of our plans, desires, wills, and emotions, for He is the way, the truth, and the life.*

Since 1945, I have fully trusted my life and soul to our Lord Jesus Christ, seeking always to rely completely upon the truth and the authority of the Holy Bible. My life has been greatly enriched as a result. His holy Word has never failed me and never will. It is encouraging and helpful, although not necessary for me, that mature leaders through the centuries also have expressed their trust in and dependence on the Bible.

Sir Isaac Newton, certainly one of the greatest scientists who ever lived, the father of mathematics and physics, said, "There are more sure marks of authenticity in the Bible than in any profane history."

Abraham Lincoln stated, "I believe the Bible is the best gift God has ever given to man. All the good from the Savior of the world is communicated to us through this Book."

And Immanuel Kant added, "The existence of the Bible, as a book for people, is the greatest benefit which the human race has ever experienced. Every attempt to belittle it is a crime against humanity."

Another reason I believe the Bible is the Word of God is that the characteristics it claims for itself are like the very attributes of the living God. My meditation and study have shown me that, like God, His Word is holy, everlasting, absolutely true, powerful, personally fair, and never changing. If it is the Word of God, it should reflect His character—and it does.

For me, the Bible is like Lake Tahoe to the millions of people who are sustained daily by its refreshing waters. As I face the so-called tough times of life, I never fail to find strength in the Bible. Daily, I draw down from the storehouse of the treasure of His Word hidden in my heart.

Let me share some examples you may well remember:

In Abraham's life I see how God challenges our faith but always keeps His sustaining promises, even if the wait is 430 years! While waiting on Him to fulfill His will, we are not to take carnal shortcuts, even if our closest and dearest love in all the world might suggest it. We wait on Him and His ways and His timing.

In Moses' life I am blessed to be reminded that age is a positive factor in following God; it is a qualifier, not a disqualifier! Moses had two complete careers before God called Him into his most important mission at age eighty. He was not ready until he had led sheep for forty years in the desert. That encourages me. How about you?

The life of Nehemiah reminds me it is never too late to finish what God has us start.

Joshua's life teaches me how important it is to daily hear, read, study, meditate on, and memorize God's Word. And take the promise that comes with it: "Then you will have good success" (Josh. 1:8 NKJV).

From Elijah I learn that we are never alone, even though we feel that way. Elijah said, " I, even I only, am left" (1 Kings 19:10 KJV). Those were his feelings, but they were not the facts of his situation. There were eight hundred other prophets of God who had not worshiped Baal.

From David I learn so much. His life, with as many terrible downs as majestic ups, reminds me that God will not turn away from any soul who has a broken and contrite heart. David showed us that there is always victory available for a man "with a heart for God." Through David's pen, as well as the words of other psalmists, the Holy Spirit taught me to sing God's praises, to know that the joy of the Lord is my strength, to expect those songs in the long nights of concern, to expect to be able to exchange the "garment of praise for the spirit of heaviness" (Isa. 61:3 NKJV). Above all, the example of loving God's Word has fortified me (Ps. 119).

From Solomon I learn the vanity of what the world has to offer. From Isaiah I understand His holiness and my lowliness, and I foresee the power of the suffering servant. From Jeremiah the prophet I learn even more what it means to weep over those who do not know our Savior.

In Ezekiel I find a diligence about the loss of a loved one: "In the evening my wife died. And in the morning I did as I was commanded" (24:18 NASB).

Habukkuk uttered the phrase that distinctly has been a rock on which I stand: "The just shall live by his faith" (2:4 NKJV).

Jonah showed how God will go to great lengths to get our attention, and there is no place so low that He cannot resurrect us to serve Him.

Malachi joyfully showed God ready to fling open the windows of heaven and pour out a blessing on all of us who will put our money where our faith is.

I will not continue here, but you surely see what I mean: every page of the Bible is an adventure with God. Do not miss it!

Relying upon all these references and my experiences in claiming the promises of God, I firmly believe the following topics are ways to demonstrate our love, trust, and obedience to our great God. The Bible specifies, among the basics of the Christian life, that every believer must know certain things. I like to meditate on the following:

- The attributes of God: "I will meditate on your majestic, glorious splendor and your wonderful miracles" (Ps. 145:5).

- The opportunity to love God "with all [our] heart, soul, mind, and strength and our neighbors as ourselves" (Matt. 22:37–39).

- The uniqueness of Jesus: He alone was virgin born, lived a sinless and a miraculous life, died a death atoning for the sins of humanity, was raised from the grave, now lives in every believer, and is coming again. He has become, for believers and unbelievers alike, the centerpiece of history. At this very moment, He is interceding for us at the right hand (place of authority) of our Father in heaven.

- The authority and reliability of the Bible as our written guide for discovering and following a holy God.

- The abundant life, given and enabled by the Holy Spirit, who is the third person of the triune Godhead. To maintain vital union with Him, I practice Spiritual Breathing: (*exhale*) I repent and confess every known sin and claim His forgiveness (1 John 1:9) and (*inhale*) by faith claim to be filled, controlled, and empowered by the Holy Spirit in obedience to Ephesians 5:18–19. (For more on this vital concept, please turn to the Appendix.)

- The power of confident prayer to the one, true, living God, who hears and answers prayer and honors fasting.

- The duty to help fulfill the Great Commission of Jesus to make disciples of all nations.

- The power of choosing to obey God and His Word in following Jesus by faith and not by feelings.

- The value of fellowship with like-minded followers of Christ to help make known the most joyful news ever announced: God loves us and offers a wonderful plan for our lives.

- The certainty that as we sow, we also will reap.

- The certainty of a Judgment Day when all will give an account for what they have done in the body on earth.

- The power of praise to our loving heavenly Father.

DECIDING TO BE DISCIPLINED

My body and spirit need nourishment. Although it is easier to feed the body than to feed the spirit, both take time and preparation. Only the Holy Spirit can prepare what I need for my spirit. But only I can place myself at the table of blessing, asking Him to nurture my spirit, confessing all known sin, asking and expecting His filling, opening His Word and reading it. And I can turn on the music created by dear musicians in the faith whose talents have been violin strings in the hands of the Master. The bow of His Spirit moves across the strings of their lives, and by Him, through them, I am elevated in spirit, reminded whose I am, seated in the heavenlies, with a perspective near to that of the Father who loves me so. Every single day I know these certainties are there. If I want them to be active in my life, I simply ask the Father.

Reading news without reading the Bible will inevitably lead to an unbalanced life, an anxious spirit, a worried and depressed soul.

In the mirror each morning, I see myself, merely one grain of sand in the oceans and beaches of the earth and eternity, and I wonder: who am I that the awesome Creator-God of the entire universe should even contemplate my existence, much less listen to my lungs breathe and my heart beat? But He *does*. And He loves me. I am on His mind and in His plans for this day. Yes, God delights in each of His children. He made us in His image. We are very important to Him.

Fear and faith cannot cohabit the same moment in the mind and soul. Faith comes by the Word of truth; that is what sets believers in Jesus apart from every other creation (John 17:17; Rom. 10:17). He did not give us any spirit of fear—none. Respect for danger? Yes.

Knowledge of threats? Yes. But frightened hearts? No. He gave us a spirit of love and the power of a sound mind (2 Tim. 1:7). He long ago began to develop that discipline in me, so I would not linger thinking upon what the enemy of our souls wants me to think, or go where the world is leading, and especially not let self—which is at war with God—set the agenda for the day (Rom. 8:7–8).

Choosing to be yielded to the Spirit is the key to living supernaturally in the kingdom of our Lord. We must be active about this choosing. Sitting back as couch potatoes and letting the world fill our minds are dangerous things. I must choose to think His thoughts or to ask Him to give me His thoughts. The world system—from the contents of the breakfast food to the news of the day—can confound and distract me from heightened awareness of His presence. There is more discouragement in a day's newspaper or fifteen minutes of television news than in the entire Bible. Reading news without reading the Bible will inevitably lead to an unbalanced life, an anxious spirit, a worried and depressed soul. By contrast, meditating upon His Word will inevitably bring peace of mind, strength of purpose, and power for living.

"A Mighty Fortress"

A mighty fortress is our God, a bulwark never failing;
Our helper He amid the flood of mortal ills prevailing.
For still our ancient foe doth seek to work us woe—
His craft and power are great, and, armed with cruel hate,
On earth is not His equal.

—Martin Luther

SEVEN

GOD'S PURPOSES IN SUFFERING

God will not look you over for medals,
degrees or diplomas, but for scars.

—ELBERT HUBBARD, 1923

As we drive the highways of life, we sometimes encounter roads under construction. A diamond-shaped orange sign inevitably declares: "Men at Work." The sign affects us. We slow down. We are watchful for new directions. We expect change to confront us. I have wondered how much differently we would look at pain and suffering if there were a sign at the scene declaring: "God at Work."

Because He *is* at work in our lives. Jesus said that the very hairs on our heads are numbered, that not even a sparrow falls without the all-seeing eye of God taking notice. Isaiah said that God scans the earth looking to bless us. God does not cease to be His loving self because we temporarily encounter dislocations and even dead ends. He is working!

Many theories try to explain why God allows suffering and pain and dying and death. But check those sources. They are poor substitutes for the all-knowing God who made us, His inspired written Word, and the magnificent Lord Jesus who was tested and suffered even as we do—yet He conquered death.

He knows that pain and suffering have significance. They have meaning as channels of experiencing grace in our lives. Our anguish matters to God. He knows our way. Our suffering also matters to the body of Christ. We are not alone in bearing up under the burdens of suffering. Paul said, "As a result, I can really know Christ and experience the mighty power that raised him from the dead. I can learn what it means to suffer with him, sharing in his death" (Phil. 3:10). But our primary Partner through pain is God, the Precious Comforter who walks beside us and goes with us through the misery. He *knows* exactly how we feel.

> *See Him on the cross dying for us, and know for yourself you have a Savior and Friend and High Priest who has been through it all for us.*

What about our pain and suffering? Whenever I experience pain or discomfort, I find it helpful to review Scripture describing our Lord's agony during His illegal trial and His cruel crucifixion and death. He was a Man of Sorrows, fully familiar with the frailties of these bodies, the torments of pain; the immense suffering literally burst His heart. See Him on the cross dying for us, and know for yourself you have a Savior and Friend and High Priest who has been through it all for us. Therefore, He understands and truly empathizes with the feeling of our infirmities. What a precious Consoler is He!

He is always our Helper, if not our escape. God walks with us through pain rather than protects us from it.

No matter what may happen to us, it is always right to look to Jesus and identify with Him and learn from His life. He is the Author and Finisher of our faith (Heb. 12:2). So, even in dying, I recommend that we identify with the Lord Jesus Christ and think of His example for us in how He died.

In Italy at the Milan Cathedral there are three inscriptions over the respective doorways. Over the right-hand door there is this motto: "All that pleases is but for a moment." Over the left-hand door the words say, "All that troubles is but for a moment." But over the central door there is this simple sentence: "Nothing is important save that which is eternal." This means that suffering, though temporal, has eternal impact and is therefore significant.

Above all, suffering has its purposes. Remember that the pain, the suffering, or the loss not only comes to pass, but it comes to pass for a purpose. Ask Job. Ask our Lord Jesus. The pain and suffering do end, and depending on our responses, God's purposes can be fulfilled. Did I say there are purposes for suffering? Is there life-value in dying? Yes, yes, a thousand times yes. God has given us in His holy, inspired Book, the Bible, great insights into suffering, testing, and faith.

Often, though we find it uncomfortable to face, the primary purpose of suffering stems from our need for self-crucifixion that the life of Jesus might live through us (Gal. 2:20). Paul said, "I die daily" (1 Cor. 15:31 NKJV). Jesus said that if we are to follow Him, the first order of the day is to "deny self" or die to self (Matt. 16:24).

I cannot describe this process any better than Charles Fenelon, a sixteenth-century bishop who wrote,

> Often, when you suffer, it is the life of your self-nature that causes you pain. When you are dead, you do not suffer. If you were completely dead to your old nature, you would no longer feel many of the pains that now bother you.
>
> Endure the aches and pains of your body with patience. Do the same thing with your spiritual afflictions (that is, trouble sent to you that you cannot control). Do not add to the cross in your life by becoming so busy that you have no time to sit quietly before God. Do not resist what God brings into your life. Be willing to suffer if that is what is needed. Overactivity and stubbornness will only increase your anguish.

God prepares a cross for you that you must embrace without thought of self-preservation. The cross is painful. Accept the cross and you will find peace even in the middle of turmoil. Let me warn you that if you push the cross away, your circumstances will become twice as hard to bear. In the long run, the pain of resisting the cross is harder to live with than the cross itself.

See God's hand in the circumstances of your life. Do you want to experience true happiness? Submit yourself peacefully and simply to the will of God, and bear your sufferings without struggle. Nothing so shortens and soothes your pain as the spirit of non-resistance to your Lord.

As wonderful as this sounds, it still may not stop you from bargaining with God. The hardest thing about suffering is not knowing how great it will be or how long it will last. You will be tempted to want to impose some limits to your suffering. No doubt you will want to control the intensity of your pain.

Do you see the stubborn and hidden hold you have over your life? This control makes the cross necessary in the first place. Do not reject the full work that the power of the cross could accomplish in you. Unfortunately, you will be forced to go over the same ground again and again. Worse yet, you will suffer much, but your suffering will be for no [other] purpose.

May the Lord deliver you from falling into an inner state in which the cross is not at work in you. God loves a cheerful giver. (II Corinthians 9:7) Imagine how much He must love those who abandon themselves to His will cheerfully and completely—even if it results in their crucifixion.[1]

Solomon stated that a brother's love was "born for adversity" (Prov. 17:17 NKJV). Paul wrote in Romans 5 that trouble in God's eyes simply sets off a chain reaction that leads to the spreading of God's love more broadly and deeply throughout our very being. This is illustrated in the way that raw iron ore becomes beautiful steel. When they pull iron ore out of a mountain, it is worth only a few dollars a ton. But after that same ore is placed in a Bessemer furnace, under tremendous heat and pressure its worthless elements, called slag, are disconnected from ideal elements that form a high grade of surgical steel of great value. Our loving God uses difficulty in our lives to burn away the sin of self and build our faith and spiritual power. Our times of trouble, heartache, and sorrow can be God's holy love refinery that makes us the kind of people that He wants us to be.

Our times of trouble, heartache, and sorrow can be God's holy love refinery.

What does God think when trouble strikes us and we cry out, "Why, God?" His sovereign Majesty is more than willing to respond, to provide a meaningful, timely reply, much of which is already written down in the Bible or lived out in the life of His Son, Jesus Christ.

Among the many possible answers to that question are these, based upon His Word: (1) this world system is fundamentally opposed to the laws and ways of God; (2) human selfishness is capable of unbelievable cruelty; (3) Lucifer and his minions work to thwart God's will (1 John 2:11–15); and (4) death is the price of a sinful, depraved nature (Rom. 3:23). However, God's love for us is absolutely unstoppable (Rom. 8:37–38).

Remember the truth I shared earlier: whatever may happen to believers has been filtered through the love of God to accomplish His purposes, which may not seem readily apparent to us at the moment, but He works them together for our good and His glory and for the extending of His love in Christ throughout the earth.

WHY THE TROUBLE, GOD?

Have you ever prayed, "God, why do good, even godly people, suffer?" I struggled with that question, and in Bible study and prayer, some clear answers came to me. Above all else, we know God is a loving God, and He wants to turn our tragedy, heartache, sorrow, and upheaval into triumph, blessing, joy, and peace.

Difficulties and suffering are tools with which He shapes us into the image of Jesus Christ. It is never fun to be enrolled in the academy of adversity, but unless God takes us through the curriculum of trials, we will never become the quality persons He wants us to be. Romans 5:3–5 explains this process. It shows adversity can become the touchstone of character.

Romans 8:28 promises, "God causes everything to work together for the good of those who love God and are called according to his purpose for them." Have you ever read on to 8:29 to discover a paramount purpose of God in troubles? "That He might be the firstborn of many brethren," Paul says. Tragedy is a platform for evangelism! God uses even the most disastrous situations for our good.

In the summer of 1976, thirty-five female Campus Crusade staff leaders—including my wife, Vonette—gathered in Colorado for a retreat. That night, they were trapped in the Big Thompson Canyon flood.

Around 1:30 in the morning, I was awakened and informed of the flood and of the rescue of one of the women, who was then in the hospital. About an hour later, another staff member was brought to the hospital by helicopter. By that time, we had good reason to believe that several of the women had drowned.

I did not know if Vonette was safe, struggling for her life in the floodwaters, or dead. But I had incredible peace because I knew that God is sovereign and ever present. So even though I had no idea where Vonette was and could not help her, I knew God was with her and the other women. Because He is all-powerful, God could save all the women whose lives were in danger. But God is also all-knowing. If it was best for Vonette to be taken home to heaven, I could completely trust my loving Father to do the right thing.

Soon I sadly learned that seven of our staff women perished during the flood. I knew that each of those women was rejoicing in the presence of her Savior. I also learned that Vonette and twenty-seven other staff women had escaped the raging water.

In the following weeks, we mourned for those dear friends we had lost. But we also felt led by God to make their last moments on earth a tribute to our sovereign God. With full approval of the grieving families, friends of Campus Crusade ministry placed full-page ads, daily and weekly, in most newspapers across the country featuring pictures of the seven women who died. The headline read, "These seven women lost their lives in the Colorado flood, but they are still alive and they have a message for you." The advertisement gave readers an opportunity to read the gospel and receive Jesus Christ as their Savior.

Approximately 150 million people read those ads. The response was phenomenal. Only God knows the full extent of what happened, but many thousands wrote to say that they had received Christ as a result of the tragic deaths of those seven women. A foreign ambassador told us that his life was changed by the ad, and he later helped open the door for ministry in his country, which had previously been closed to the gospel.

We can give all our worries and cares to God, knowing that He cares about what happens to us. When tragedy strikes, take comfort in the fact that no difficulty will ever come into your life without God's permission. Knowing this truth does not make adversity pleasant, but it gives us hope that the result will be worth whatever pain we endure.

Through the years, an associate and I began to go further in asking God why troubles and trials befall us. Here are some of the insights God showed us. Hear God lovingly answer our question: "Why the trouble, God?" I would like to distinguish between *causes* of suffering and *purposes* in suffering. The distinction may not be obvious, but some troubles derive from ungodly causes, while others—such as Job's afflictions—come with God's permission. Technically, He can make all things work together for His purposes, but let's first look at some causes.

SOME CAUSES OF TROUBLE

Why, God? *Because I love you and have a plan for you to examine yourself privately and correct your ways to align with My requirements so that I will not have to judge you publicly* (1 Cor. 11:28–30). For some, this is God's holy warning system. Wake up to the sin in your life, confess and repent, and seek the filling of the Holy Spirit. Otherwise, what you have sown privately will be reaped publicly. We are to examine ourselves, not judge others as did Job's critics—something Jesus specifically warned against (Matt. 7:1–3).

Why, God? *Because I love you and I want you to understand a fundamental principle of My world: you reap what you sow* (Gal. 6:7). I know it is not fashionable to say so these days, but sometimes our suffering is the harvest of our choices. This inevitable truth finds us out. The good news is that if we sow love and peace, obedience and faith, those, too, shall we reap.

Why, God? *Because I love you and I want you to be patient with all people, even as I am patient with you* (James 1:2–3). Impatience is a sign of immaturity. God is patient. So sometimes God allows troubles to grow patience in us. We are His children, and we should act like it.

Why, God? *Because I love you and you are resisting My plan for order, not chaos, in this world. You cannot be at peace in this world if you rebel and fight against the authority chain I have established* (Col. 3:17–23; 1 Tim. 2:2). My friend Bill Gothard has taught this truth so well. If only young and old could realize that submitting to authority releases God's blessing in our lives.

Why, God? *Because I love you and I cannot have fellowship with you while you have unconfessed sin in your life* (Ps. 66:18–19; 1 John 1:8–9). Mankind seems so slow and unwilling to accept this truth: God is holy, pure, and totally sinless. We should shriek at sin the way some do at the sight of mice or snakes or hornets. God hates sin. So must we.

Why, God? *Because I love you and have chosen to use you as a key agent in executing My redemptive strategy for the world—and I needed to get your attention to be able to communicate this to you* (John 20:21). This great truth is readily seen in the lives of Moses, Joseph, Daniel, Philip, and Paul. One thing about being laid down is that it is much easier to look up. Have you accepted your wake-up call?

Why, God? *Because I love you and I wanted you, by virtue of the loss of your loved one, to have an inkling of just how much I loved My Son and you* (John 3:16; 14:29; Gal. 6:2). The intense grief of being separated from our loved ones is a brief glimpse of how much the Father grieved at the moment the Son went to Calvary and bore our sin. When we "weep with those who weep," we also are beginning to realize how much God loved us in sending His Son to die for us.

Why, God? *Because I love you and I wanted to see how much you love Me—as much as or more than the things of this world* (John 13:15; 1 John 2:13–16)? Every day, I find countless opportunities to decide whether I will obey God and demonstrate my love for Him or try to please myself or the world system. God is waiting for my choices.

> *When we "weep with those who weep," we also are beginning to realize how much God loved us in sending His Son to die for us.*

SOME PURPOSES OF SUFFERING

Why, God? *Because I love you and plan to use your experience to serve as a guide or model for others* (1 Cor. 10:11; Heb. 11:11–39; Phil. 4:9). The entire eleventh chapter of Hebrews illustrates how God uses human followers as examples to encourage us in our faith, even those who died for following the Lord Jesus. Are you in trouble? Someone is watching how you handle it. The sermon of your life in tough times ministers to people more powerfully than the most eloquent speaker.

Why, God? *Because I love you and I will comfort you—making you able to comfort others who experience the same kind of trouble, which will encourage them* to come to Me due to the very real empathy you will be able to give them (2 Cor. 1:3–7, 9; Heb. 2:18). This great truth demonstrates how God can work the worst together for His glory, our good, and the good of others.

Why, God? *Because I love you and have chosen you as a witness in this world—even as I sent My own Son—and you can expect some of the same kind of trouble He experienced* (Matt. 5:11–12). We are, after all, Christians, Christ-ones, and if there is not some crisis between us and the anti-God world system, then we really should be surprised.

Why, God? *Because I love you as My very own child and would not dare let you grow and develop undisciplined, wild, as though you had no parent to nurture you* (Heb. 12:5–13). Any loving parent knows this truth. Chaos and anarchy are born in the homes where children are not disciplined. Growing up with no respect for authority, they ever push the limits as adults, and society spends billions on the tragic consequences, from police to courts to prisons.

Why, God? *Because I love you and I do not want you to grow up criticizing others, lest you place yourself in the line of My judgment that I would have to administer to you with the same standards and intensity you judged others* (Matt. 7:2; Rom. 14:4, 10–12). This truth should stop our mouths of condemnation and increase our prayers for others.

Why, God? *Because I love you and I want you to remember that you are just one of My children, each of whom I love, each of whom has trouble, each of whom has access to My rescue services* (1 Cor. 10:13). We can look around, and usually, we can find someone who has a situation worse than ours. Someone has suggested that the very moment we think our trials are unique, look out, the enemy of our souls is ready to pounce. We are not alone in our testings; others have it worse. Others have passed this way, sought His grace, and moved on. So can we.

Why, God? *Because I love you and have planned that your life will be used to bring others to a knowledge of Me; in this way My Son, who suffered so much to carry out the plan of redemption, will be honored and surrounded by an eternal family* (Rom. 8:28–30). Perhaps the richest example of this point is the young missionary Jim Elliot, who was killed by the Auca Indians he sought to reach with the love of Christ. His life and testimony were so profound that his killers came to Christ and world missions has been forever fueled by his faith-filled words, written in his personal diary October 28, 1949: "He is no fool who gives up what he cannot keep to gain what he cannot lose."[2] The faithfulness of his wife and family has held high the flame of his torchlight of truth.

Why, God? *Because I love you and I want you to learn to obey the Father, trusting in His intelligent, comprehensive plan for your life* (Heb. 5:8). This decision must be made a thousand times over until it becomes an attitude of faith. Trials and sufferings teach us to obey the Lord by faith, and we soon learn that obedience pays in joyful ways.

Why, God? *Because I love you and I have a growth process for you, which—to the world's confounding—starts when you are at your worst and brings you into a knowledge of My best* (Rom. 5:3–5). This is why we can thank God when we encounter trials and sufferings. God immediately begins to work His grace in us in a wonderful equation that produces more of His love in our lives.

Why, God? *Because I love you, I am listening for your plea, and I will come to your side to help you get through this experience* (Heb. 4:16). When you are in physical distress, do you call 911? God's holy Word is filled with emergency help and testimonies. David, the king of Israel, said, "I waited patiently for the LORD; and He inclined to me, and heard my cry" (Ps. 40:1 NKJV), and "The LORD will strengthen him on his bed of illness; You will sustain him on his sickbed" (Ps. 41:3 NKJV).

Why, God? *Because I love you and have chosen to honor you with the special opportunity to see My Son ascended, as did Stephen in his martydom. Though the price of this experience is the end of your human life, your witness will have a dramatic impact on others who will spread the gospel with new fervency* (Acts 7:56–60). Some die as martyrs. It was reported that as many as 145,000 died as martyrs in 2002 throughout the earth because of their faith in Christ. Being ready to die is the main thing. God can be glorified in the worst.

Why, God? *Because I love you and I want you to draw your encouragement exclusively from Me; don't expect the world system to provide you with this encouragement* (John 16:33). Why do we expect to be refreshed by most of what comes out of Hollywood or other entertainment and pleasure centers? Only the sweet fellowship of kindred minds in Christ encourages us. God sometimes allows troubles so that we will learn that only His encouragement really makes a difference.

Why, God? *Because I love you and I have a plan to use your life experience to bring glory to Myself and teach others at the same time* (John 9:1–3). God has a plan for each of us, and for some it involves what appears to be unpleasantness, disability, and/or disfigurement. Evangelist David Ring, for one example, has cerebral palsy, and he has demonstrated for the world that God can use disease and disability to communicate His love. Ring humbles us with his admonition: "Kwitchyourbellyachin'."

> *As self is set aside in obedience, the Savior can reign with special blessings to you*

Why, God? *Because I love you and I want you to grow up mature; this requires less of you and more of Me* (2 Cor. 11:24–30; 12:9–10). Paul said, "I die daily." John the Baptist explained, "He must increase and I must decrease." As self is set aside in obedience, the Savior can reign with special blessings to you (John 14:21).

Why, God? *Because I love you, and I want you to be happy and content, which is achievable by trusting only in Me* (Phil. 4:11–13). Oh, how easily we let the little things of life spoil the joy of our salvation. But we can obey our Lord's command: "Seek first the kingdom of God and His righteousness, and all these things [the 'stuff' of this world that we may need] shall be added to you" (Matt. 6:33 NKJV).

Why, God? *Because I love you, and when I see you at the end of your life, I want you to really enjoy the occasion of coming into the complete fullness of the salvation planned for you in heavenly ceremonies since the beginning of time* (1 Cor. 3:11–14; 1 Peter 1:6–9). God is not surprised that hurts come. Trials on earth prepare us for the joys of heaven. He is working it out. Just seeing Jesus our Savior in heaven will be worth it all.

Why, God? *Because I love you and want you to fully realize that nothing can keep Me from loving you—nothing, not this situation or any to come, not now, not ever* (Rom. 8:37–38). Someone said the only things that are certain are death and taxes; that is false. Death may be avoided by the Rapture or the return of Jesus to the earth. Taxes are always levied but not always collected. But neither death nor taxes nor anything in life—except our selfish wills—can come between you and God's care. God and His love stand forever—unchanging, unyielding, always saying, "I love you" from Calvary and "I can help you" from the empty tomb.

Why, God? *Because I love you and have strategies to defeat your enemies, and to keep you, bless, and reward you for being faithful while under attack. Trust Me while I work out these matters* (Isa. 41:10–13; 54:11–17; Rev. 21:4–7). We can always trust God to have a better idea than the enemy or than our own schemes. But it is a challenge to "wait upon the Lord."

Why, God? *Because I love you and I wanted you to be reminded I am the only One you can trust to lead you in this world to total and meaningful life and peace* (John 10:2–5). Others will let us down, forsake us, criticize and condemn us. To our peril, we place our trust in them or in our own strength. To our prosperity, we trust God.

This collection is but a drop in the river of God's love, which we can understand as we study His holy Scriptures. Let us not be like the Pharisees whom Jesus admonished because "you don't know the Scriptures, and you don't know the power of God" (Matt. 22:29).

It is surely true that when we have some understanding of how God is working in our lives and how our troubles fit into His plan, it is much easier to accept difficulties. Place the sign upon your soul today: "God at Work."

"Amazing Grace"

Amazing grace! How sweet the sound—that saved a wretch like me!
I once was lost but now am found, was blind but now I see.

Through many dangers, toils, and snares, I have already come.
'Tis grace hath brought me safe thus far, and grace will lead me home.

—John Newton

EIGHT

TWO STARK TRUTHS

Yes, what joy for those whose record the Lord has cleared
of sin, whose lives are lived in complete honesty!

—KING DAVID (PS. 32:2)

*I*n this period of sickness, in what are probably my final earth-bound days, I am more aware than ever of two realities: the first to emerge is the dark depravity and utter unacceptability of my sinful self before a holy God, and the second is the wonderful, embracing love and mercy of our Savior.

I am not alone in this realization. In 1847 Sir James Simpson of Edinburgh discovered the use of chloroform as an anesthetic in surgery. At that point in history, it was considered the most significant discovery of modern medicine. In his later years, he was asked, "What do you consider to be the most valuable discovery of your lifetime?" Without hesitation he said, "My most valuable discovery was when I discovered myself a sinner and that Jesus Christ was my Savior."

Most Christians do not know or fully realize that the adversary of our lives is Satan and that his main tool is our flesh, our old nature. Let us name the scoundrel within—it is the self, the ego. The old self rebels against God and will twist and turn anything and anyone to try to preserve itself. Yet Jesus said, "He who saves his life will lose it." As we yield ourselves to the selfish nature, our lives develop cancers in the eyes of God. You can watch the self as it demands attention, seeks its own way, insists on vain recognitions of this world, works to build little monuments to itself, manipulates people to make itself look good, neglects to spend time with God or loved ones, and indulges itself with food and leisure and pleasure. If we are yielded to the Holy Spirit, we will not do these things—yet we do not yield to Him, and we do the wrong things. Why?

The flesh (and its nature) is not neutral; it is at war with God. It is impossible to please God doing things motivated by and produced by the flesh (Rom. 8:7–8). A rock may as well try to be a rose. While love in the Holy Spirit "does not seek its own," the flesh never seeks anything except its own (1 Cor. 13:5).

An illustration of this process is just below many lawns in Florida where there are two water systems: one is the good municipal water system, and the other is the owner's well-water pump. Most lawn sprinkling systems are able to use either one through the feature of a pressure valve. Many people turn on their own water pumps, which are strong enough to override the municipal system and to pull their own groundwater through the pressure valve to water their lawns. If they did not do that, the pressure valve would naturally give way to the much more costly municipal system, which gives better water because it comes from a better source and has been treated to kill parasites. So the tendency is usually to cut back on "the good stuff" and let the owner's cheaper well-pump water flow on the yard.

That same kind of tendency is in our hearts as we too often reduce our reliance upon the power of the Holy Spirit. Instead we turn to our natural flesh (as pictured by the home-based groundwater) and let it govern the days of our lives. Before God, we, too, must look as brown, dying grass, soon to wither away.

SINFUL SELF

One of the great tragedies of life is the persistent and virulent disease of self-ishness. It beckons me to seek my own way, to try to bargain new deals with God and man, and to do the very things that I know do not please God.

What a depraved rascal Bill Bright is in the old man![1] With the hymn writer, I say, "My sinful self my only shame; my glory all the cross."[2]

The key for me lies in the intimate conversation our Lord Jesus had with His disciples: "If any of you wants to be my follower, you must put aside your selfish ambition, shoulder your cross, and follow me" (Matt. 16:24). Several translations say, "Deny self."

That command of our Lord flies directly in the face of the Western materialistic, hedonistic value system that grips us and threatens to engulf Christianity itself. The first command of the world system is this: "Gratify self now." The second command of the world system is like it: "Sacrifice anything and anyone for self-indulgence."

For example, and this is an indictment, not a mere instance, surveys show that a high percentage of Western men, including pastors, are gripped by addiction to pornography. They must have it, even at the expense of their marriages, their call, their walks, and their reputations. It is Satan's powerful tool of the times to destroy the sacred joy of marriage, to shatter families, and to break God's commands.

Do we realize what Jesus said about lust? "You have heard that the law of Moses says, 'Do not commit adultery.' But I say, anyone who even looks at a woman with lust in his eye has already committed adultery with her in his heart" (Matt. 5:27–28). For a man, it is one

> *For a man, it is one thing to observe the beauty of God's created woman, but it is quite another to take a second look of lust.*

thing to observe the beauty of God's created woman, but it is quite another to take a second look of lust that consumes the mind at the expense of a husband's sexual drive for his own wife.

This beast within us is spectacularly selfish. It will buy boats and trucks and clothes and houses and lands so that people will look at us and say nice things, while our children suffer without time, attention, clothing, and educational support—and while spouses try to make do on pocket change for necessities. It will spend money a family does not have to grasp for worldly values that do not satisfy. As a result, we are slaves to debt, not to God. When we stand before God, as we all will, do we really think we are going to say: "What do You think of my SUV? Don't You agree it's nicer than my truck?"

What a contrast with our Lord Jesus' command to set aside selfish ambition. He used word pictures later cited by Paul to convey the taking off of old, filthy clothes and the putting on of new, clean robes to walk in holiness: "Put on the Lord Jesus Christ, and make no provision for the flesh in regard to its lusts" (Rom. 13:14 NASB).

We may know Galatians 5:22–23 and its wondrous glow: "When the Holy Spirit controls our lives, he will produce this kind of fruit in us: love, joy, peace, patience, kindness, goodness, faithfulness, gentleness, and self-control. Here there is no conflict with the law." But do we realize how to obtain that fruit of the Spirit? The very next verse tells us the first step: "Those who belong to Christ Jesus have nailed the passions and desires of their sinful nature to his cross and crucified them there" (Gal. 5:24).

Paul plumbed this problem further:

Do not let sin control the way you live; do not give in to its lustful desires. Do not let any part of your body become a tool of wickedness, to be used for sinning. Instead, give yourselves completely to God since you have been given new life. And use your whole body as a tool to do what is right for the glory of God. Sin is no longer your master, for you are no longer subject to the law, which enslaves you to sin. Instead, you are free by God's grace. (Rom. 6:12–14)[3]

LOVING SAVIOR

The second reality that is more evident to me now than ever before is the transforming, powerful, and precious love of our Savior. Since I opened my life to the living Lord in 1945, I have been in love with Him. But let there be no mistaking it, I love Him not because I think it is a good idea and the right thing to do. No, my best motives are not worthy of His love. I love Him because He first loved me, and He still does love me, and He will love me forever and ever. While I am still prone to be impressed with my sin-sick self, I do not want to dwell on it further because the very act of doing so is self-centered. The love of God, by contrast, overwhelms me with acceptance, forgiveness, compassion, and joy in believing.

What an incredible love is His! Can you hear His voice today, saying, "I love you. Why? Because I want to! Before the world began I chose you. I laid aside My glory and became a human sacrifice for you. I gave up My life for you. There is nothing you can need that I cannot supply. Bring your little cup of need to My great river of sufficiency and be refreshed. Don't you see? It is I who loves you, your God, Creator of the universe, Sustainer of life, Savior, and Lord"?

God, of course, is love, and love is the attribute of God that has always captivated me. I first felt the spark of God's love in my saintly mother. But it was not until I realized how unlovely I was that it began to dawn on me how great is God's love for me. He came all the way from the comfort and beauty of heaven to the blood-stained cross of Palestine, not just for someone like me in the theoretical, but for precisely me in the personal and practical. He rescued me from sin's darkness. He ransomed me from the hostage cell of hell. He gave His life in exchange for mine. His love is beyond grasping—but not beyond receiving (Col. 1:13–15). And He did the same for you.

It is no wonder that David the psalmist would write, "From the rising of the sun unto the going down of the same the LORD's name is to be praised . . . Great is the LORD, and greatly to be praised . . . while I live will I praise the LORD" (Ps. 145:3; 113:3; 146:2 KJV)

He came so far and stooped so low, it truly is hard to conceive. I recall talking with a brilliant student from India, who had two doctorates in the sciences. He believed in reincarnation and that all life was sacred, but he could not understand God's love and forgiveness. He could not grasp why God would reveal Himself to man in the person of our Lord Jesus Christ.

Another brilliant person, Solomon, said, "Consider the ant." Perhaps that was in my mind as I suggested that this Hindu student think of God and humanity this way: "If you saw an anthill about to be destroyed, how would you communicate with the ants to warn them of impending doom?" The student shook his head. I suggested shouting and writing and stomping would not succeed. The student saw the truth and said, "You would have to become an ant!" "Yes," I said, "and that is why God in Christ came to be human, in order to communicate the danger of sin and then to die on the cross to rescue us from the certain punishment we deserve."

A Native American who had lived a rough life came to Christ through the witness of a missionary. He also found it hard to describe the love of God he was experiencing. He gathered friends together and bent down. He found a worm, picked it up, and placed it on a pile of leaves. Then he took a match and set the leaves on fire. As the flames drew nearer to the center where the worm was, the old chief plunged his hand into the burning pile and snatched out the worm. Holding the worm gently in his hand, he said, "I . . . that worm!"

One of our great hymns, "At the Cross," originally spoke of God's love "for such a worm as I." The writer of those words was the gifted Isaac Watts. President Thomas Jefferson thought Watts's lyrics were so outstanding, he ordered that the government pay for the printing of his lyrics in a book as required reading for the students of the District of Columbia.

But by 1956, Watts's "worm" must have offended someone's sensibilities because it was changed in one hymnal to read, "For sinners such as I." Let me say again: it was not until I realized how *unlovely* I was in the eyes of a holy God that I came to understand *how much* He really loves me. I, a worm. He, the great Lover of my soul.

The transforming love of God has repositioned me for eternity. I am now a new man, forgiven, seated in the heavenlies, basking in the warm love of our living God, trusting His promises and provision, and enjoying life to the fullest.

"THE LOVE OF GOD"

The love of God is greater far than tongue or pen can ever tell;
It goes beyond the highest star, and reaches to the lowest hell;
The guilty pair, bowed down with care, God gave His Son to win;
His erring child He reconciled, and pardoned from his sin.
O love of God, how rich and pure! How measureless and strong!
It shall for evermore endure the saints' and angels' song

—F. M. Lehman

As the years have passed, I have sensed even more fully four aspects of God's love:

1. Its *condescension*. He loved us even while we were yet sinners at war with Him!

2. Its *completeness*. In Him we have everything we need, the very fullness of the Godhead.

3. Its *communion*. He cried over Lazarus, and He cried over Jerusalem, and He wept for all of lost humanity, and yet His first words on the cross were: "Father, forgive them!" What love is this?

4. Its *constancy*. He is the same yesterday, today, and forever, and His unchanging and unfailing love sustains me when nothing and no one else can.

With the hymn writer William Newell, I sing,

> Oh, the love that drew salvation's plan.
>
> Oh, the grace that brought it down to man.
>
> Oh, the mighty gulf that God did span at Calvary.
>
> Mercy there was great and grace was free.
>
> Pardon there was multiplied to me.
>
> There my burdened soul found liberty, at Calvary.

God is the source of all love. It flows out of the great reservoir of His goodness. In fact, God's love never fails. The psalmist declared, "The LORD is good. His unfailing love continues forever" (Ps. 100:5).

Unlike human love, God's love is pure and holy, and while people are sometimes willing to violate standards of honesty, righteousness, and morality in order to please others, God never compromises any of His attributes or standards.

Out of God's abundant love, He offers us grace. It is because of God's loving grace that Jesus died on the cross for our sins so we could experience an eternal relationship with Him: "The LORD is gracious and compassionate, slow to anger and rich in love" (Ps. 145:8 NIV). There is nothing we can do to make God love us any more or less. He loves us because He is gracious, not because of who we are, but because of who He is.

God's supernatural love is perfect and unconditional. The psalmist proclaimed, "How priceless is your unfailing love!" (Ps. 36:7 NIV). For most people love centers on what they themselves are receiving from the relationship. He loves us because He is God and we are His creation. It is His nature to love. His is a never-ending love, a love that will not be terminated because of disappointment or a change of heart. It is a love that we can count on for all eternity.

As John wrote, "We need have no fear of someone who loves us perfectly; his perfect love for us eliminates all dread of what he might do to us. If we are afraid, it is for fear of what he might do to us, and shows that we are not fully convinced that he really loves us" (1 John 4:18 TLB).

God demonstrates His love by His sacrificial commitment to our well-being. God's love involves sacrifice. John declared, "This is how God showed his love among us: He sent his one and only Son into the world that we might live through him. This is love: not that we loved God, but that he loved us and sent his Son as an atoning sacrifice for our sins" (1 John 4:9–10 NIV).

How much a person loves someone is obvious by how much he is willing to sacrifice for that person. Jesus gave His life on our behalf. He could not have sacrificed any more. His love for us is supreme. The apostle Paul wrote to the church in Rome: "I am convinced that nothing can ever separate us from his love. Death can't, and life can't. The angels can't, and the demons can't. Our fears for today, our worries about tomorrow, and even the powers of hell can't keep God's love away. Whether we are high above the sky or in the deepest ocean, nothing in all creation will ever be able to separate us from the love of God that is revealed in Christ Jesus our Lord" (Rom. 8:38–39).

God's love involves wanting what is best for us. Paul asserted, "We know that in all things God works for the good of those who love him, who have been called according to his purpose" (Rom. 8:28 NIV).

Contrary to the way humans are inclined to think, love is not soft and mushy, timid and tame. God's love is firm and resolute. During the hippie era of the sixties, "love" was a sensual road show of drugged concerts. To counter that period's view, a friend wrote,

> Love is not a rolling stone
> That gathers no moss.
> No, love is God away from home
> Dying on a Cross.

Such love compels me to want to give sacrificially to others. A Navajo woman, who had been cured of a serious ailment by the medical treatment of a missionary doctor, was greatly impressed by the love he manifested. "If Jesus is anything like the doctor," she said, "I can trust Him forever."

So can I. Would you like to know for sure you can trust Him too? Please turn to Appendix A and read "Would You Like to Know God Personally?"

"TRUST AND OBEY"

When we walk with the Lord in the light of His Word,
What a glory He sheds on our way!
While we do His good will, He abides with us still,
And with all who will trust and obey.
Trust and obey, for there's no other way
To be happy in Jesus, but to trust and obey.

—James H. Sammis

NINE

THE HOME STRETCH

I strain to reach the end of the race and receive the prize for which God, through Christ Jesus, is calling us up to heaven.

—THE APOSTLE PAUL (PHIL. 3:14)

I enjoy the Olympics, especially the discipline and courage of track and field runners. There is a point in every race that rivets our attention. It is in that final segment of the contest when every athlete somehow finds more strength to excel. For marathon runners it comes after grueling hours of paced struggle. For sprinters it is the last second's burst for the finish line.

In either case there is a last lap, a final stretch, an ending to one's labors. But I applaud those who never quit serving our mighty God as long as they have an ounce of strength or a fleeting breath. One such royal servant of our Lord was William Booth, founder of the Salvation Army. At age eighty-two and almost blind, before an audience of ten thousand at Royal Albert Hall in London, he uttered these last public words:

While women weep as they do now, I'll fight.
While children go hungry as they do now, I'll fight.
When men go to prison, in and out, I'll fight.

While there is a drunkard left, I'll fight.

While there is a poor girl left on the streets, I'll fight.

While there remains one dark soul without the light of God, I'll fight.

I'll fight, I'll fight to the very end.[1]

The apostle Paul used the example of runners to describe the Christian life:

> Remember that in a race everyone runs, but only one person gets the prize. You also must run in such a way that you will win (1 Cor. 9:24).

> Hold tightly to the word of life, so that when Christ returns, I will be proud that I did not lose the race and that my work was not useless (Phil. 2:16).

He disregarded his very life to complete his course: "I do not consider my life of any account as dear to myself, in order that I may finish my course, and the ministry which I received from the Lord Jesus, to testify solemnly of the gospel of the grace of God" (Acts 20:24 NASB).

He even urged us to run the whole race and not drop out:

> Since we are surrounded by such a huge crowd of witnesses to the life of faith, let us strip off every weight that slows us down, especially the sin that so easily hinders our progress. And let us run with endurance the race that God has set before us (Heb. 12:1).

I see myself as being in the home stretch, and as I make decisions, I am testing them by Paul's wonderful claim: "I have fought a good fight, I have finished the race, and I have remained faithful" (2 Tim. 4:7).

Like most knowledgeable believers, I, too, look to the moment when the Lord Jesus will say, "Well done, good and faithful slave." But this is not the primary motive for me. Rather, I press forward because He loves me so much, and I love Him in return.

GOAL SETTING

Vonette and I have always set goals. Our most important time of goal setting was when we literally signed contracts with God in 1951. We were specific in turning over every area of our lives to His ownership and control. We decided to live as slaves of Jesus, and it was the greatest decision we have ever made. We set goals as slaves of Jesus: to give Him our possessions, our finances, our family, our dreams, our best. Vonette focused on practical matters such as a home suitable for the famous, yet welcoming to the homeless. She aimed at opportunities to travel, speak, and write. I basically signed over my business and my plans to the Lord. We would live day by day and talk with Him constantly about how to live. Approximately twenty-four hours later, the Lord gave me His vision for my role in helping to fulfill the Great Commission in this generation, Campus Crusade for Christ International. I firmly believe that without our contract surrendering all to God, I would not have received the vision for the ministry He gave us. Countless are the goals we have set in seeking to be obedient to that vision. And I weep at the faithfulness of God in all that He has allowed us to see Him do.

It is important to set goals because if you do not have a plan, a goal, a direction, a purpose, and a focus, you are not going to accomplish anything for the glory of God. One of the sad things I have witnessed today is that people are afraid to take a chance, lest they lose favor with

> *I firmly believe that without our contract surrendering all to God, I would not have received the vision for the ministry He gave us.*

their friends. So, sadly, they dumb down their vision. When a vision is merely palatable to a crowd, it requires no act of God.

My policy has always been to ask God to help me set goals because I believe God has a plan for every person. I like to set goals based on Philippians 2:13: "For God is working in you, giving you the desire to obey him and the power to do what pleases him." If I am totally yielded to Him, informing my mind with His Word, and trusting in His Holy Spirit to help me obey His commands and trust His promises, I claim by faith that the promptings of the Spirit I experience are, in fact, His directions.

Many people say, "I've never heard God speak." Could it be they are so busy and the world they are in is so loud, they simply cannot hear God? As I write this, I am in a room with a television, a radio, a telephone, a fan, a CD player, and a DVD player. Guess what? None of them is on.

I focus on God, His attributes, His Word, and I listen for His Spirit's promptings. I converse with other followers of Christ and listen for His thoughts conforming with His Word and my own mind's recollections of how He works. Occasionally, I do turn on some blessed worship songs, and I love to hear the great hymns of the church, vocally or instrumentally. And I also enjoy such great Bible teachers as Charles Stanley, Adrian Rogers, John Hagee, David Jeremiah, and the ministries of Pat Robertson, Jerry Falwell, and Paul and Jan Crouch of Trinity Broadcast Network.

Paul said, "I am sure that God, who began the good work within you, will continue his work until it is finally finished on that day when Christ Jesus comes back again" (Phil. 1:6). He counted upon God to initiate and to accomplish: "Faithful is He who calls you, and He also will bring it to pass" (1 Thess. 5:24 NASB).

I have been cautioned not to state goals in specific numbers because if you do not reach those numbers, somebody will consider you a failure. This advice has come from world-renowned figures whom I admire. But I like to set specific God-given goals because, first of all, I am a slave of Jesus, and I do what my Master tells me to do. Sometimes God may tell us to set a goal we may not reach, even with His help. Sometimes I may not have understood Him fully. Sometimes my zeal has outpaced practical wisdom. For example, I was about twenty-seven when I proposed that Billy Graham speak at the Los Angeles Coliseum. That was about 1947, and Dr. Graham had yet to become recognized, but I knew God's hand was upon him. So I went to the coliseum, which then could hold about ninety thousand people. The manager listened patiently to me and asked me to come back a week later. Then the manager and board rightly questioned my experience and refused my request. Of course, since that day Billy has spoken to millions.

But I want to help stretch people, I want to help their faith grow, and I want to help their vision expand. So for more than fifty years, I have set numbers and deadlines out on the cutting edge. Doing that can be risky, of course.

I believed God wanted us to see 100,000 Christians spend one week in discipleship and evangelism training at the first-of-its-kind conference we called Explo '72 in Dallas, Texas. My critics lamented that we had only 85,000 workers at Explo '72. But that turned out to be the largest number of Christians trained for an entire week in history to that point. During the week, the Cotton Bowl was nearly filled. Each evening, about 85,000 came, and overflow crowds of approximately 280,000 attended the last day in a nearby park.

Now, I do not pluck figures out of the air. I ask God to show me. I pray that He will continue to cleanse me from unrighteousness and surround me in such a way with His presence that the only thoughts I have are those filtered through His blood, His Word, His presence, and the Holy Spirit and those that are His will. So, I will think only His thoughts.

By faith, then, as I live throughout the day, I have to believe the thoughts that enter my mind are from Him because early in the morning I have surrendered my mind to think His thoughts, my heart to love with His love, my will to do His will, my lips to speak His truth, my hands and feet to serve Him. With that commitment, I believe that when ideas come—and they are in conformity with His will revealed in the Bible—

then those ideas are from Him. His Holy Spirit within me witnesses with my spirit that the ideas came from Him.

A slave does not have a reputation. I am just doing what God tells me to do, and I let Him defend me. Jesus said, "The truth is, anyone who believes in me will do the same works I have done, and even greater works, because I am going to be with the Father" (John 14:12).

If that is true, and it is, then we ought to talk about it. I think it is an insult to God not to think supernaturally. Set goals so big that unless God helps you, you will be a miserable failure.

I am all for being culturally sensitive and doing things wisely, decently, and orderly. But the church can get so caught up in man-centered managing and political correctness that it forgets to envision what God can do.

> *Set goals so big that unless God helps you, you will be a miserable failure.*

Our main duty as believers is to proclaim the good news of Jesus through evangelism and discipleship. I have witnessed how easily most organizations can be diverted from their foremost goals and objectives.

Goals are worth setting and worth missing. We learn from nonsuccesses. But unless there are a vision and an entrepreneurial spirit, most organizations turn a corner down a dead-end path. We need to always ask: What can God do in this? Will we fail unless God intervenes?

The same thinking should apply to us as individuals and families. Are we achieving only what we can accomplish in our own strength? If so, that is of the flesh and does not honor God. I often have heard people say, "Well, I'm doing the best I can." Where is the faith in doing only what we can? Let us be willing to say to God: "Here I am; I surrender all of me. Lord, do all You want to do in and through me."

Permit me to encourage you to aim high. Decide to finish strong. And then love, trust, and obey God, and ask Him to help you complete the race, looking unto Jesus.

THE EXAMPLE OF SAMUEL

Samuel had been a judge of all Israel, its leader. But the people decided they wanted a king, and Samuel graciously stepped aside to begin what may well be the greatest legacy of his entire life: "It came to pass, when Samuel was old . . ." (1 Sam. 8:1 KJV). He did not retire. He became a powerful prayer intercessor and a trainer of young believers, saying, "God forbid that I should sin against the LORD in ceasing to pray for you; but I will teach you the good and the right way" (v. 12:23).

Praying and teaching—not retiring! I never intended retirement, and I am so grateful to God that He has kept my mind active in more than eighty major book and video projects since terminal disease struck my life. I long have felt that even if I am further restricted in my activities, I can go around the world for my Lord by interceding in prayer for others, especially for leaders.

Dr. V. Raymond Edman, a past president of Wheaton College, said,

> In my opinion, Samuel did more for Israel in the days of retirement than in all the long years of active and conspicuous service. He prayed for people and their new king in days that were darker and more difficult than any they had known under Samuel's administration . . . The Divine Record states succinctly: "Moses and Aaron among his priests and Samuel are them that call upon his name, they called upon the Lord, and he answered them."[2]

A VISION IN THE NIGHT

While lying in the hospital recently, I had a dream. Samuel's example may have been on my mind. In this dream I believe God gave me a special message to the multitudes of older people all over the world. Some call us senior citizens. And some call us elderly or seasoned citizens or prime timers. I answer to all four, especially at supper.

In this vivid dream I was allowed to identify with other older, dear people, all over the world, many of whom are infirm, confined, and immobile. I felt what they felt. I thought what they thought. I hurt where they hurt. I felt the hopelessness of many and the helplessness of others. This applies to many who are reading these words now.

Many feel that their work is finished, that there is nothing left to be accomplished. Some feel that there is no future for themselves. Many feel that they are just waiting to die. They want to go and be with Jesus, yet God has put in all humans the will to live, so as with the apostle Paul, they are "betwixt" the two (Phil. 1:23 KJV), wanting to go, yet wanting to stay.

Even many healthy people feel as though their accomplishments are all behind them and they are no longer of value to God, to their families, or to society. They feel they are just marking time until God takes them home. Some are engrossed in hobbies to pass the days, usually harmless, but not related to God's purposes in the earth.

When I awakened from my dream, I had a clear impression of this message that God gave me to give to older or disabled people:

Your loving heavenly Father has not forgotten or given up on you. He knows who you are, where you are, how you are, and what you are doing. He still has work for you to do! As His Word says, it is His will that you continue to bear fruit in old age (Ps. 92:14). He wants me to share with you how He wants to bless and use you.

Whether you have twenty years left, ten years, one year, one month, one day, or just one hour, there is something very important God wants you to do.

Whether you have twenty years left, ten years, one year, one month, one day, or just one hour, there is something very important God wants you to do that can add to His kingdom and your blessing. He has called you to this hour. He has prepared you for this task. This is your destiny.

I am eighty-one and no longer in the fast lane. But Christians never retire from being servants of our great Creator-God and Savior. We are never too old to be in business with and for the King of kings. Feelings of uselessness and hopelessness are not from God, but from the evil one, the devil, who wants to discourage you and thwart your effectiveness for the Lord.

But, believe me, God wants to use you! Your life and mind are valuable to Him, and we all are still accountable to Him for how we spend our days.

HOW GOD CAN USE YOU

Though I am in bed and on oxygen twenty-four hours each day, I am experiencing one of the most fruitful periods of my life. Whether or not you are mobile, there is even something greater you can do. Yes, I said greater!

Some readers might be able to do many other things, but there is one role any believer can aspire to: you can serve God in the high calling of a prayer intercessor! There is not a more important job in the body of Christ than that of an intercessor. Prayer intercession provides the power and foundation for everything else that is done, for the Lord God says, "Call to Me and I will answer you, and I will tell you great and mighty things, which you do not know" (Jer. 33:3 NASB).

You can be a prayer intercessor while in a bed or a wheelchair. You can do it literally anywhere. If you do not have the strength to pray aloud, you can whisper it. If you cannot whisper, you can move your lips. If you cannot move your lips, then pray silently, in your mind. God knows and reads your heart. Remember what God says: "The earnest prayer of a righteous person has great power and wonderful results" (James 5:16).

To intercede means "to pray for," "to plead," "to entreat," "to stand in the gap for another." This is a high and holy enterprise. We are joining in a task that engages the Father, Son, and Holy Spirit.

We know that:

> The Holy Spirit helps us in our distress. For we don't even know what we should pray for, nor how we should pray. But the Holy Spirit prays for us with groanings that cannot be expressed in words. And the Father who knows all hearts knows what the Spirit is saying, for the Spirit pleads for us believers in harmony with God's own will. (Rom. 8:26–27)

Of Jesus it is written: "He is able . . . to save forever those who draw near to God through Him, since He always lives to make intercession for them" (Heb. 7:25 NASB).

In the Old Testament, the Levitical priest stood between man and God; he represented man to God. But now, Jesus is our High Priest, and in the New Testament, all believers are priests (Rev. 1:6). You can exercise your priestly role and stand before God, pleading and interceding for others.

Your humble prayers can actually help change the world!

Your humble prayers can actually help change the world! You may touch millions of lives and maybe even help change nations. The apostle Paul asserted, "When I am weak, then I am strong" (2 Cor. 12:10). Are you weak? Then by faith, with Paul, declare that you are strong! God is in you and wants to work through you!

Sometimes God uses His power to anoint talented men and women to raise up huge international ministries that may touch millions or even billions of souls, and we thank God for them. But most times that same power will rest simply on one humble person, a person who in the world's eyes may seem weak, lowly, foolish, and totally without influence. Yet with God's

Spirit operating in and through that person, he or she has access to all the supernatural power of the universe! Such a humble person, without pride and ego, is qualified to receive God's power, actually more than a person self-confident in his own abilities. The Bible confirmed:

> God chose the foolish things of the world to shame the wise; God chose the weak things of the world to shame the strong. He chose the lowly things of this world and the despised things—and the things that are not—to nullify the things that are, so that no one may boast before him. (1 Cor. 1:27–29 NIV)

As a Spirit-filled follower of Jesus, even in that hospital bed or in that bed or chair of confinement at home or in a nursing home, you are a temple of God—a container of God's power, the same power that raised Christ from the dead: "If the Spirit of him who raised Jesus from the dead is living in you, he who raised Christ from the dead will also give life to your mortal bodies through his Spirit, who lives in you" (Rom. 8:11 NIV). That power is described by the Greek word *dunamis*, from which we get the word for dynamite. The people around you may not know it, but you are an explosion waiting to happen!

Like dynamite, God's power is only latent power until it is released. You can release God's dynamite power into people's lives and the world through faith, your words, and prayer.

WHAT TO PRAY FOR

Always pray according to God's Word. Pray His Word back to Him, in faith. When we pray His Word, we know we are praying in His will, and "if we ask anything according to his will, he hears us. And if we know that he hears us—whatever we ask—we know that we have what we asked of him" (1 John 5:14–15 NIV).

Here are some things for which you can pray according to God's Word:

- Pray by name for the salvation of family members and acquaintances (2 Peter 3:9).

- Pray blessings for family members, acquaintances, churches, and ministries. (The Bible is filled with blessing Scriptures; see: Deut. 1:11, 26:15, 33:16, 24; 1 Samuel 1:11; 1 Chron. 4:10, 17:27.)

- Pray blessings for any enemies or anyone who may persecute you or not treat you right (Luke 6:28).

- Pray for governmental and other leaders (1 Tim. 2:1–4). Your prayers can literally change the course of nations. God says that He wants us to pray for them "that we may live peaceful and quiet lives in all godliness and holiness" (v. 2 NIV).

- Pray for national and international revival and righteousness (Prov. 14:34).

If you are not sure what to pray for or how to pray, just ask God to show you. He will. The Spirit helps us in our weakness. We do not know what we ought to pray for, but the Spirit Himself intercedes for us with groans that words cannot express.

FASTING

If you are physically able, consider combining fasting with your prayers, a biblical discipline. You may want to fast one meal a day or more. Since 1994 when I was age seventy-three, I have been led each year to conduct a forty-day extensive water and juice fast, which God has greatly used. I would encourage you to do the same. But there are precautions. Do not do it legalistically; do it only as the Holy Spirit leads. Do not fast if you have medical problems, which, in my case, have prevented me from a forty-day fast so far this year. Even if you are in relatively good health, you should consult a doctor. (You may want to read a book for advice about fasting, such as my book, *The Coming Revival*.)

Prayer Changes Things

When I was only a young man in 1947, God put it on my heart to pray for the former Soviet Union. I do not know why. I had never even been there. It was just something the Lord led me to do in His wisdom and sovereignty. I prayed for that nation for decades without ever seeing any results.

Then in the 1980s, President Mikhail Gorbachev was riding the crest of popularity and great power as head of the atheistic Soviet Union. But President Gorbachev was only a man, and God's Word tells us, "The king's heart is in the hand of the Lord" (Prov. 21:1 KJV).

Our Russian representative living in the Soviet Union at the time, Dan Peterson, was teaching in a very prestigious school for the children of ambassadors. Dan communicated with my wife, Vonette, and me that we should organize a twenty-four-hour, thirty-day prayer vigil and encourage Christians all over the world to pray for the liberation of the Soviet Union. Vonette was then chairperson of the international Lusanne intercessory prayer committee, a Billy Graham ministry to millions. She sent a plea to Christian leaders around the world, representing millions of believers, to pray that God would do something dramatic and supernatural to liberate this nation, calling others to intercede in prayer for that thirty-day period.

Russia had previously known nine hundred years of Christianity, but for seventy-three years had been under the oppressive, anti-God Communists. We felt strongly led by the Holy Spirit that we should pray that the people of the Soviet Union would be liberated out of their bondage.

Then in God's incredible timing, I saw one of the most dramatic answers to prayer that I have ever observed. The thirty days passed, and miracle of miracles, on the very first working day following those thirty days of prayer, President Gorbachev announced new freedoms through what were called *glasnost* (openness) and *perestroika* (restructuring). That was the beginning of the end of the Soviet Union and the beginning of religious freedom for a nation of nearly 300 million people. There has since been an explosion of the gospel in Russia and all of the former Soviet Union through Campus Crusade for Christ and other ministries.

Many people prayed, but it could have been the added prayer of a single, little, weak, humble prayer warrior who turned the tide and made the difference. God often orchestrates prayer, involving many people. If one person had failed to pray, possibly an infirm senior citizen, the results might not have been the same.

> *It could have been the added prayer of a single, little, weak, humble prayer warrior who turned the tide and made the difference.*

There is no doubt that prayer literally influences men and nations in accordance with God's promises and purposes. Ask the Holy Spirit to give you a similar burden and leading for our country or another nation or group of people. Maybe it will be China, South Asia, Africa, Europe, South America, or some other country or area. When He does, obediently step out in faith with it, pray, ask and keep on asking, and believe God's promises.

God will hear and answer, according to His own plans and divine timing. And you will be an important part of that plan.

FROM MY HOSPITAL BED

In 2001 the prayers of my many friends and family began to be answered, and I have enjoyed a remarkable two-year extension of my life. By miraculous circumstances, the Lord sent into my life a Russian doctor who uses alternative medical techniques, and my breathing and my stamina began to greatly improve, unexplainable by conventional medicine. Even though, as I mentioned previously, I require tanks of oxygen twenty-four hours a day, God has enabled the past two years to be among the most productive of my life as I have been able to keep a vigorous schedule of writing, editing, producing teaching videos, and even some traveling and speaking until the past several months.

Many people thought I would be gone from this world by now. The situation reminds me of that of Mark Twain, who, after reading his obituary in a newspaper, laughed off the erroneous report and stated, "Rumors of my death have been greatly exaggerated."

Of course, even if the Lord tarries, my day to enter glory will eventually come. What a wonderful day that will be! Only God knows how much time I have left, and I rest peacefully in His loving, capable hands. It is a win-win situation for me. If I go, I will be with my wonderful Lord, whom I have served, and with other loved ones. If I stay, I will be able to joyously serve Him even more. But as long as I am here, as long as I have breath, I will serve the Lord.

"Find Us Faithful"

We're pilgrims on the journey
Of the narrow road
And those who've gone before us line the way
Cheering on the faithful, encouraging the weary
Their lives a stirring testament to God's sustaining grace
Surrounded by so great a cloud of witnesses
Let us run the race not only for the prize
But as those who've gone before us
Let us leave to those behind us
The heritage of faithfulness passed on through godly lives.

Oh may all who come behind us find us faithful
May the fire of our devotion light their way
May the footprints that we leave
Lead them to believe
And the lives we live inspire them to obey.

—Jon Mohr

FINAL INSTRUCTIONS

Then when Jacob had finished this charge to his sons,
he lay back in the bed,
breathed his last, and died.

—MOSES (GEN. 49:33)

nowing for sure your time on earth is short speeds your thinking. You want to be certain you are prepared for eternity. And you want to leave things in the best order possible. I confess I was slow to give proper attention to some of these "final directives," as the lawyers call them. Most Americans die without wills, leaving their assets to be ravaged by the courts or wrestled over by relatives. That is a sin: "Those who won't care for their own relatives, especially those living in the same household, have denied what we believe. Such people are worse than unbelievers" (1 Tim. 5:8).

God has given me the grace and the time to handle these matters. Caring for our families can sometimes seem a task too big for us; that is because it *is* too big for us. Balancing that obligation is the wonderful news that all believers have everything we need "in Christ." "For this is the secret: Christ lives in you, and this is your assurance that you will share in his glory" (Col. 1:27), and "You are complete through your union with Christ. He is the Lord over every ruler and authority in the universe" (Col. 2:10).

I cannot personally provide for every single need of my family, but God can. And their needs are to be met in the completeness of being united with Christ. We must remember: "It is God who works in you both to will and to do for His good pleasure" (Phil. 2:13 NKJV), and "He who calls you is faithful, who also will do it" (1 Thess. 5:24 NKJV). God asks that we do our best in faith and let Him handle the rest. It is astounding how many burdens we can generate for ourselves by thinking we are somehow the center of the universe. Instead, we should obey what is plain, pray much, and trust God completely to work things together for our good and His glory (Rom. 8:28).

Would you like to give a great gift to your family? I wish to do so to the extent that I can by handling basic and natural tasks. I do not wish to leave burdensome tasks for my family if I can simply communicate some final instructions, or perhaps I should say instructions about final things on this earth for me. The Bible paints this word picture for us: "Timely advice is as lovely as golden apples in a silver basket" (Prov. 25:11).

As did other patriarchs, Jacob spoke of each child and made his final preparations:

> Then Jacob told them, "Soon I will die. Bury me with my father and grandfather in the cave in Ephron's field. This is the cave in the field of Machpelah, near Mamre in Canaan, which Abraham bought from Ephron the Hittite for a permanent burial place. There Abraham and his wife Sarah are buried. There Isaac and his wife, Rebekah, are buried. And there I buried Leah. It is the cave that my grandfather Abraham bought from the Hittites." Then when Jacob had finished this charge to his sons, he lay back in the bed, breathed his last, and died. (Gen. 49:29–33)

DIFFICULT DECISIONS

The toughest decisions in life are said to be those involving death. Hard medical choices are posed by the so-called advancements of human technology and modern medicine. There are marvels that can jump-start and jolt a part of the body into functioning when it really does not want to do so. George Washington told his physician, "Doctor, I am tired of dying."

Before I go a step farther, let me clarify: I oppose any notion of euthanasia—the concept that a committee or a code by law somehow decides when a person should die. That is God's decision. For the same reason, I believe it a sin to commit suicide, though it is not the unpardonable sin. As followers of Jesus, we are to love life and care for our bodies but not worship the body of this life. We are to seek to preserve the body until it is clear that the body God gave us is simply worn out or subjected to external forces beyond our control.

Pastors tell of the pummelings taken by their parishioners as various machines shock and mechanically attempt to continue functions that the body, if left alone, would simply stop.

NO DETOURS, PLEASE

I want to die as if it were 1903, not 2003. I have signed the necessary papers to this end. (Each state has different laws for which your doctor or attorney can supply the paperwork.) I do not want heroic or extraordinary measures taken by the medical community as I leave this life. I am on my way to a better life, and I do not want to be waylaid or detoured by the admirable but distracting technologies of the twenty-first century. I say "distracting" because compared to the glory of heaven and the physical presence of Jesus, they are as nothing.

To make this abundantly clear, I have asked that no one call 911 in the event I am taking one of my last gasps. Why? Because paramedics are under legal obligations to try to prolong life as best they can and with all their skills. I do not want this much fuss and bother. I would much prefer to be looking into the eyes of any one of my beloved family or friends than to be sailing through a stoplight with a siren blaring and various devices stuck in me, trying to keep me alive.

> *I want to cross the great divide as naturally and supernaturally as possible. Letting the body die in its natural way. Letting my soul soar in its supernatural way.*

I want to cross the great divide as naturally and supernaturally as possible. Letting the body die in its natural way. Letting my soul soar in its supernatural way. And I have great peace about the journey. I let Paul speak for me:

We know that when this earthly tent we live in is taken down—when we die and leave these bodies—we will have a home in heaven, an eternal body made for us by God himself and not by human hands. We grow weary in our present bodies, and we long for the day when we will put on our heavenly bodies like new clothing. For we will not be spirits without bodies, but we will put on new heavenly bodies . . . as a guarantee he has given us his Holy Spirit. So we are always confident, even though we know that as long as we live in these bodies we are not at home with the Lord. That is why we live by believing and not by seeing. Yes, we are fully confident, and we would rather be away from these bodies, for then we will be at home with the Lord. (2 Cor. 5:1–8)

As a younger man, I felt this way by faith in the authority of God's holy, inspired Word. Now, I am experiencing its truth as if by sight. It is abundantly clear to me that God's way includes a season for everything: "A time to be born and a time to die" (Eccl. 3:2).

There are appointments with God: "It is destined that each person dies only once and after that comes judgment" (Heb. 9:27). In this life I have kept some appointments, rescheduled some, and missed others. I may be one who is blessed to miss the appointment with death because the Lord returns first. My appointment may be postponed by a healing from the hand of God. But I am ready to keep my appointment with death more cheerfully than I have any of my appointments in the past.

Dear friend, make as many "final decisions" as you reasonably can. Take the pressure off your family by expressing your wishes about the following:

- Your assets in a will.

- Your memorial celebration service with your family and in a letter or consultation with your pastor.

- Conversations with, and perhaps a note to, your spouse.

- Your faith in a written declaration.

- Your funeral and burial expenses by transactions before the fact. (You can save your family thousands of dollars and much grief this way. There are simple funerals, and there are simply outrageous, ornate undertakings. I want to keep mine simple.) I remember President Dwight D. Eisenhower chose, as a matter of conviction, to be buried in an ordinary G.I. (government-issue soldier's) coffin. And he was, except someone added a red suede lining.[1]

- Your personal effects in the will or by letter, thereby saving family very difficult decisions.

ONE ON ONE

A pastor in Florida tells of receiving a call from a man dying of cancer. The gentleman, a Christian, was in a lot of pain, and he knew he had very little time. He asked, "What should I do?"

The pastor, after covering the basics I have cited above, offered this suggestion: "Ben, why don't you call in your wife and children—one at a time—and just talk? Share your faith. Bless them. Have a prayer with them. It will be good for each one and for you. Don't make this a group thing. Let it be personal, one on one."

Within three weeks the man died, but in the intervening days, he made and kept those appointments with each one near and dear to him. His testimony lives on. This is biblical, as seen in the actions of the patriarchs of the Old Testament and of our Lord Jesus Himself. I have followed this advice, even videotaping individual messages to my dear Vonette, each of our children and grandchildren.

Communication is so important. When I have found myself out of fellowship with someone, I have examined my heart, and I have tried to live by "The 12 Words" that God gave me for family relationships:

- I was wrong.

- I am sorry.

- Please forgive me.

- I love you.

As we end our journey here on earth, some behavioral experts list a need for words to be spoken about forgiveness, love, thanksgiving, and farewell. There may well be a need for final transactions. For example, in his last days the father of a dear friend said to his son, "I'm sorry." "What for, Pop?" "All those dumb financial decisions I made," said the father. "Oh, Pop, you're forgiven; we all make mistakes, and the Lord has that under control." But my friend said his father's confession "meant very much to me" in helping heal old wounds in the family.

A helpful question to ask yourself is: How do I want to be remembered by my loved ones? This question came vividly to the mind of Alfred Nobel when he opened the newspaper one morning to read his name in the obituary column under the headline "Dynamite King Dies." Yes, the newspaper got it wrong; it was his brother who had died. But it disturbed Alfred that he might be remembered solely for his inventing new ways for packaging and using dynamite. What about his other interests in life? So he founded the Nobel Prizes for advancement in various fields, including the acclaimed Nobel Peace Prize.

The point is, he stopped to assess his life and determined what legacy and reputation he would leave behind. It affects how you will die. It sets your priorities. You may decide to go witnessing rather than refining your golf swing. You may want to set up a trust or scholarship fund instead of anxiously watching the stock market. As for me, I want to be praising our great Creator-God and Savior when I die, looking forward to heaven and the day of reunion that will occur for our family there, while in the meantime telling everyone who will listen about Christ. Since I have shared virtually all of these things with my family, they know how I feel, and I believe I have relieved some of the pressure they might otherwise have had to handle.

"All Hail the Power of Jesus' Name"

All hail the power of Jesus' name!
Let angels prostrate fall;
Bring forth the royal diadem,
And crown Him Lord of all;
Bring forth the royal diadem,
And crown Him Lord of all!

Ye chosen seed of Israel's race,
Ye ransomed from the fall,
Hail Him who saves you by His grace,
And crown Him Lord of all;
Hail Him who saves you by His grace,
And crown Him Lord of all!

—Edward Perronet

JOY THROUGH IT ALL

I am filled with comfort;
I am overflowing with joy in all our affliction.

—PAUL (2 COR. 7:4 NASB)

*A*re you experiencing joy? Is joy part of your walk? I have never forgotten the words of the New Testament scholar James Stewart of Edinburgh, Scotland: "If we could but show the world that being committed to Christ is no tame, humdrum, sheltered monotony, but the most exciting adventure the human spirit can ever know, those who have been standing outside the church and looking askance at Christ will come crowding in to pay allegiance . . . And we may well expect the greatest revival since Pentecost."

I have been thrilled to learn that this great professor of the gospel never wavered as he reached the end of his days on earth. Because he was widely respected, he often was asked to conduct funeral services for believers. For the surviving family, he advised: "When you pray and your faith is strong, you are holding on to the left hand of the Risen Christ. Your loved one who has gone before you into eternal life now holds on to the right hand of the Risen Christ. In the meantime, Christ is your bridge. Hold fast!" In his own last hours, he was asked his condition, and he replied, "I'm just waiting here to venture forth into God's next great adventure."[1]

JOY IN PERSPECTIVE

Jesus said as we obeyed Him, our "joy might be full" (John 15:11 KJV). Nehemiah proclaimed, "The joy of the Lord is my strength." Joy, indeed, comes from a Person, but we can also discover it when our minds are in a place of peace where that Person is in control. It is all about perspective. Let me illustrate.

Nestled in the heart of the Ozark Mountains is Joy—Joy, Arkansas. Let me suggest that this little town symbolizes the mind-set of a Christian with a right view of life and of God. It has some distinctive characteristics:

- In Joy, you have a tremendous perspective, overlooking valleys and mountains and streams and pastures, more than 240 degrees of view.

- In Joy, as a result, you can see trouble or triumph coming for miles; you can see storms on their way and those that have passed by.

- In Joy, you can look all around you and see the handiwork of the great Creator-God, and it is all good.

- In Joy, you can smell the clean pine scents and the fresh air tinged with fresh mountain springs.

- In Joy, you know who your neighbors are, and you check on them for caring's sake as they check on you.

- In Joy, there is freedom from crime, no stoplights, not even a stop sign.

- In Joy, there is a quiet that only nature can give.

- In Joy, the environment is pure. The polluters cannot poison the water because Joy already is upstream!

The right and complete view of our lives is, ultimately, what gives us the happiness we all seek. Ironically, the little community of Joy is located between Quitman and Rose Bud. Those are symbols we can use, too. If we place ourselves there—between the decision to quit the old man in us and turn to the Rose of Sharon, the Lord Jesus—then we can all be in Joy! Pure, spiritual Joy in Arkansas or "any state" wherein we can be content as the apostle Paul declared (Phil. 4:11).

Now, I must admit, you will not stumble upon Joy. You must purpose in your heart and mind to go there. It really is not on the way to anywhere in particular. It's not on the beaten path of this twenty-first-century culture. And it really would help you enjoy Joy if you personally knew someone who lives there.

For the follower of Christ, this kind of perspective was made available by Him, and Paul actually commanded us to gain this perspective: "Since you have been raised to new life with Christ, set your sights on the realities of heaven, where Christ sits at God's right hand in the place of honor and power. Let heaven fill your thoughts. Do not think only about things down here on earth. For you died when Christ died, and your real life is hidden with Christ in God. And when Christ, who is your real life, is revealed to the whole world, you will share in all his glory" (Col. 3:1–4).

We are seated in the heavenlies; therefore, being "okay under the circumstances" is really just an admission we have unconfessed sin or have failed to be filled with the Holy Spirit. As I have suggested, joy is the direct result of having God's perspective on our daily lives and the effect of loving our Lord enough to obey His commands and trust His promises. Jesus told His disciples: "In the world you will have tribulation; but be of good cheer; I have overcome the world" (John 16:33 NKJV). Paul reminded us: "Whatsoever is not of faith is sin" (Rom. 14:23 KJV). So we can walk in joy by faith in and obedience to our Lord.

In this human experience of living in the home stretch of life, there is the option—a studied choice, really—for me to experience a holy prizing of the very presence of God. I can choose to treasure His presence and clutch it close to my heart. I do not cling to physical life; I am claiming the manifestation of His eternal life to be more alive in me than ever. This abundant life began when I invited Him into my life to be my Lord and Savior, and it made me a new creation who will live forever (John 1:12, 10:10; 2 Cor. 5:17).

"As the deer pants for the water brooks, so pants my soul for You, O God," David stated (Ps. 42:1 NKJV). "Blessed are those who hunger and thirst for righteousness," the Lord Jesus said (Matt. 5:6 NKJV). So when I choose to think on Him, I know from His Word that He loves and enjoys my doing so. He loves it! And there also is His specific promise: "Thou wilt keep him in perfect peace, whose mind is stayed on thee" (Isa. 26:3 KJV). Hymn writer Isaac Watts penned these words: "Stayed upon Jehovah hearts are fully blest; finding as He promised perfect peace and rest."[2] Solomon said that as a man thinks in his heart, so is he (Prov. 23:7 KJV). As a grandfather, I delight in the choices my grandchildren make as they run to me for a joyous hug, an exuberant embrace. How much more does God relish the moments we run to Him! We choose joy as we choose to obey God, and our Lord keeps His promise: "When you obey me, you remain in my love, just as I obey my Father and remain in his love. I have told you this so that you will be filled with my joy. Yes, your joy will overflow!" (John 15:10–11).

There lies the choice: I can focus either on Him or on my body filled with disease. Which shall it be? The choice is easy, is it not? To gaze upon the God of love with the eye of the mind and heart is far better than to focus on the run-down, battered body of this earthly existence!

To recognize that He delights in me and the obedience I give Him by faith stirs me to delight more and more in Him. This relationship has been given many terms and, indeed, entire denominations built on the basis of a covenant or partnership between the follower of Christ and the God of creation and Calvary. I became aware of this concept among others while cramming three years of seminary into five years of studies! I have known it to be true since my walk with the Lord first began in 1945. But now I am experiencing it in a new and fresh way that only gives me further evidence of His faithfulness and the obedience He expects. I say once more, with the consequences of dying as my witness: there is no such thing as a disobedient, happy Christian; and there is no such thing as an unhappy, obedient Christian!

That may seem too glib, but let me explain. This happiness I know is a combination of internal stability, eternal security, maturity, and integrity. I am at peace; I have a certain knowing and assurance that God is with me and heaven is my home; I can depend on the promises of a holy God who made me in His image and loved me so much that He gave His only begotten Son to die for my sins and to be raised from the dead to attest that "whoever lives and believes in Me shall never die" (John 11:26 NKJV). I know from experience that joy is more than feeling good. And I depend on the integrity and the faithfulness of God to make each moment as meaningful as He can and I allow.

In fact, this is the God-blessedness I know—and any Christian can know—which includes purpose, peace, power, and the very presence of God in this life with a positive assurance of its getting better and better and lasting forever in heaven to come. This is the happiness I am experiencing.

THE PATH OF JOY

I long ago decided to believe in, trust, and rely upon the God of the Bible, and to love and obey Him as a result. He is the God whose awesome mind is searching the whole earth for those who will receive Him and the blessing He intends. He is the Creator-God of 100 billion galaxies and trillions and trillions of microscopic molecules on earth. He is everywhere, all-powerful, and all-knowing—never surprised, always consistent (2 Tim. 2:11–13). His promises are the keys to His kingdom. "Heaven and earth pass away, but my words shall not pass away," the Lord Jesus assured us (Matt. 24:35 KJV).

By fixing my mind on Him and His words, I gain His perspective. It changes how I feel about everyone and everything, including dying. Let me try to explain.

First, and above all, it starts with the object of our faith—the loving Mastermind of the universe, the Creator and Redeemer. I never want to displace Him as my first love. (It is possible that my dying days and hours are an opportunity to tell Him and demonstrate to Him exactly that I do love Him, first, last, and above and through it all.)

My motive is to love Him in return for His great love for me. I know that He is a God of love and justice, but He especially is a God of faith: "Without faith it is impossible to please [God], for he who comes to God must believe that He is, and that He is a rewarder of those who diligently seek Him" (Heb. 11:6 NKJV). Think of that! He promises to give rewards to those who never stop seeking Him! I must conclude that faith—totally depending on Him—is the secret unlocking the power of His promises. God is sensitive to our every need. He is keeping a record according to our faith-based actions, and He responds to them every single time. He is totally trustworthy; I can depend on Him when all else may falter. And if my own candle of faith flickers in the storms of life, I can ask Him to place His hand around it, to protect and sustain it. He will definitely say, "Yes," to that request. He will cause my mind to recall His promises, for "faith comes by hearing, and hearing by the word of God" (Rom. 10:17 NKJV).

Second, if I do love Him, I will obey Him, Jesus said (John 14:15). In my own strength I could not obey all His commands; that's humanly impossible. "But with God all things are possible," so I choose to believe that He who has "begun a good work in [me] will perform it until the day of [His appearing]" (Matt. 19:26; Phil. 1:6 KJV), and "I know whom I have believed, and am persuaded that he is able to keep that which I have committed unto him against that day" (1 Tim. 1:12 KJV). These days, "that which I have committed unto him" specifically includes the dying process.

Third, the joy of the Holy Spirit is experienced by giving thanks in all situations. It's not easy, of course, but it is a choice. God said, "In everything give thanks; for this is the will of God in Christ Jesus for you" (1 Thess. 5:18 NKJV). Anyone can decide to obey that. If your "obey-er" seems broken today, ask God to forgive you for that fact and to give you help to trust and obey Him as you pray a prayer of thanksgiving to Him—even though you do not feel like thanking Him. In that faith-filled and fateful transaction, you will experience the grace of God. It is how I have lived, and it is how I am dying.

But all this is not to gratify self or to set a stoic example. A stiff upper lip cannot sing praises to God; it draws attention to the creature, not the Creator. No, the act of obedience while dying is for a much deeper purpose. Listen to the promise of the Lord Jesus Christ: "He who has My commandments and keeps them, it is he who loves Me. And he who loves Me *will be loved by My Father*, and I *will love him* and *manifest Myself to him*" (John 14:21 NKJV, italics added). Here, then, is a major purpose in suffering: it gives me the opportunity to focus my obedience to and faith in Him, and as a result, He manifests—makes real, makes special, reveals, shows, and presents—His very presence to me! Joy is an inevitable result.

> *A stiff upper lip cannot sing praises to God; it draws attention to the creature, not the Creator.*

I feel inadequate in trying to make clear this process and its magnificent benefits. It is perhaps like the unleashing of nuclear power. Someone in authority needs only to push a button or throw a switch, and awesome forces are manifest—power is released, energy arrives, life-changing occurs, whether in radiation treatments or in a bomb. A simple act delivers astonishing impact. At the same time, God's manifestation of Himself is as tender as a mother's caress, the kiss of your lifelong marriage partner, or the aroma of the finest perfume.

Lastly, I have discovered this equation: the joy of God is experienced as I love, trust, and obey God—no matter the circumstances—and as I allow Him to do in and through me whatever He wishes, thanking Him that in every pain there is pleasure, in every suffering there is satisfaction, in every aching there is comfort, in every sense of loss there is the surety of the Savior's presence, and in every tear there is the glistening eye of God. After all, as noted earlier, He cares enough that He keeps our tears in a bottle (Ps. 56:8)!

Of course, it is absurd to try to oversimplify the inexhaustible riches of our complex and incomprehensible, almighty and sovereign God; yet He sat with a child in His arms and said that in the simplicity of childlike trust, great faith and power are released. So, merely to help us focus our minds, I offer these statements as keys to dying grace:

- Thanking God demonstrates faith.

- Obeying God demonstrates love.

- Praising God demonstrates joy.

As I thank Him in the tangled web of cords from electronic devices that are a part of my final surroundings, I am acting in the belief that He will keep His promises; this is faith. As I obey His commands, He plainly has said, this is love for Him. As I praise Him and not myself or my circumstances, I am liberated to focus on His presence, and this is great joy! "Bless the LORD, O my soul; and all that is within me, bless His holy name!" (Ps. 103:1 NKJV). "The joy of the LORD is [my] strength" (Neh. 8:10 NKJV).

THE BEST IN THE LAST!

Everything God promises is available to us if we obey His commands and meet the conditions of His promises! For example, He says, "Delight yourself . . . in the LORD, and He shall give you the desires of your heart" (Ps. 37:4 NKJV). I have longed for the time to write in brief and at length about the great God we know and love. In these last years of pain and suffering, He has kept His promises, every one, to refine me, to assure me, to enable me, to be with me, to bless me, indeed, to manifest Himself to me. It is an act of simplicity to choose to believe God, but it also is an act of profound complexity as God literally moves in wondrous ways throughout the universe to keep His word.

This entire home stretch is a joy for me to be able to intercede, write, and record as He inspires me. It is the fulfillment of a lifelong goal to have this time, which I must admit I might not have set aside had not our sovereign God allowed doctors to order me to slow down. There is great joy in this perspective on the temporary illness God has allowed until He calls me to His next assignment.

"Because He Lives"

God sent His Son, they called Him Jesus,
He came to love, heal, and forgive;
He lived and died to buy my pardon,
An empty grave is there to prove my Savior lives.
Because He lives I can face tomorrow,
Because He lives all fear is gone;
Because I know He holds the future,
And life is worth the living just because He lives.

—Gloria & William J. Gaither

TWELVE

KEY TO EVERYTHING

*If there is one word above another that will swing open the eternal gates,
it is the name of JESUS. There are a great many pass-words and
by-words down here, but that will be the countersign up above.*

—DWIGHT L. MOODY

*W*hen our journey is restricted, memory becomes a wonderful companion. And I have been recalling, as you might imagine, some of my many journeys with our Lord. I was remembering a trip to the Holy Land and the joy of walking in the very places where Jesus walked. Someone asked, "Of all the places in the life of Jesus, where would you most like to pause and meditate?"

The answer came quickly: "The empty tomb," I said. "It is the key to everything." Without the resurrection of Jesus there would be no basis for Christianity. So our journey together will sidetrack somewhat as we take a long look at the significance of the empty tomb of Jesus of Nazareth. Without the certainty of His resurrection, we would come to the end of this life without hope, with nothing to anticipate except despair and doubt. But because He lives, we rejoice, knowing soon we will meet our Savior face to face, and the troubles and trials of this world will be behind us.

The empty tomb means everything to me. During the early 1980s I was in Israel with a group of our board members and other friends, including Bunker and Caroline Hunt, who had financed the *JESUS* film, which was produced in Israel, directed by John Heyman and based solely on the Gospel of Luke. We were touring the spots where Jesus walked, and it occurred to me after I arrived in Israel that we should have brought the *JESUS* film with us, which we had not done. I called around and found a copy in the hands of a Southern Baptist missionary. He came over and showed it to us in one of the hotels where we were staying. All of the people who were in our travel group were really thrilled with the movie that has since become the most viewed and most translated in history.

> *I was expecting to have some kind of a great emotional experience . . . "He is not here. He is risen."*

It happened that I was invited by the late Bishop Goodwin Hudson, a leading, internationally known Anglican bishop who was the head of the Garden Tomb committee, to speak on Easter morning at the empty tomb in the garden. I went early and sat in the empty tomb, personally expecting some stunning spiritual moment. After all, there I was in the very tomb where, quite likely, the body of our Lord lay when He was taken from the cross before His resurrection.

As I sat there meditating, I was expecting to have some kind of a great emotional experience. I did not. I waited and waited and prayed, and then a still, small voice came to me, *He is not here. He is risen and is as available to every believer wherever he or she is in the world as He is here in this garden tomb.* That was a confirmation of the fact that wherever believers are, there is Jesus indwelling them. It was more than what I needed. I then spoke on the Resurrection and its certainty, and the Holy Spirit of God blessed. The entire episode was a most moving experience as the whole garden was filled with people from many countries of the world. We all had a deep sense that God blessed our time together in Israel, but the highlight was when we visited the empty tomb and realized, all afresh, with our own eyes, that it is empty! Jesus is alive, and He has given us a commission to take His message to the ends of the earth so that hundreds of millions, yes, of billions more, would become temples of the living Christ and spend eternity with Him.

The empty tomb destroys religions and glorifies Jesus of Nazareth as the Creator-God and Savior of the world. It is a simple place that presumes His virgin birth, sinless and supernatural life, soul-saving death and burial. There the most life-changing, world-shaking words ever spoken came from an angel on that early Easter morning: "He isn't here! He has been raised from the dead, just as he said would happen. Come, see where his body was lying" (Matt. 28:6). And followers of Christ have been repeating those glorious words ever since.

> When you are weary, my friend, go to His tomb.
> When you are discouraged, go to His tomb.
> When you are defeated by sin, go to His tomb.
> When you wonder if your work is in vain, go to His tomb.
> When you face dying and death, go to His tomb.

His tomb remains empty. There is no body in the grave of Jesus Christ. You can go to the tombs of the pharaohs, to the tomb of Muhammad, to the tomb of Confucius, to the tombs of religious prophets and leaders. In those tombs are their bones.

But in the tomb of Jesus Christ, there is nothing. His body is not there. Christianity is the only belief that draws millions of pilgrims each year to line up to witness an empty room.

The empty tomb is the evidence that unbelievers must face. How else can anyone

When you wonder if your work is in vain, go to His tomb.

> *The Son of God was hanged on a cruel Roman cross until, literally, His heart gave out and He died, paying the price for our sin and our shame.*

explain why a handful of timid souls, cringing in fear of the mighty Roman Empire and the tight grip of the organized Jewish religion, would go forth shouting even at the threat of their own martyrdom: "He lives. He is risen. The tomb is empty. See where they laid Him"?

Never has such silence spoken so loudly and clearly. Its emptiness hushes skeptics and testifies beyond the shadow of a doubt, as the apostle Peter said, "They [Crucifixion and Resurrection] were not done in a corner" (Acts 26:26). The Son of God was hanged on a cruel Roman cross until, literally, His heart gave out and He died, paying the price for our sin and our shame. Buried in a borrowed tomb, He was raised from the grave, just as He said He would. "For I, the Son of Man, must suffer many terrible things," He said. "I will be rejected by the leaders, the leading priests, and the teachers of religious law. I will be killed, but three days later I will be raised from the dead" (Luke 9:22).

SCHOLARS HAVE LONG VERIFIED THE RESURRECTION

C. S. Lewis posed the great trilemma: "A man who was merely a man and said the sort of things that Jesus said wouldn't be a great moral teacher. He would either be a lunatic on the level with a man who says he's a poached egg—or else he would be the devil of hell; you must take your choice." I stand with the third option: that He was and is everything He said He was, the living God.

As an agnostic in my quest for truth concerning the resurrection of

Jesus, I discovered that many noted scholars have believed, and do believe, in its historical authenticity. After examining the evidence for the Resurrection given by the gospel writers, the late Simon Greenleaf, an authority in jurisprudence at Harvard Law School, concluded, "It was therefore impossible that they [the early Christians] could have persisted in affirming the truths they have narrated, had not Jesus actually risen from the dead, and had they not known this fact as certainly as they knew any other fact."

Dr. William Lyon Phelps, a professor at Yale University for forty years and one of the most distinguished educators in the history of our country, wrote, "It may be said that the historical evidence for the resurrection is stronger than for any other miracle anywhere narrated."

John Singleton Copley, recognized as one of the most brilliant legal minds in British history, commented, "I know pretty well what evidence is, and I tell you, such evidence as that for the resurrection has never broken down yet."[1]

"I claim to be an historian. My approach to the Classics is historical. And I say that the evidence for the death and the resurrection of Christ is better authenticated than most of the facts of ancient history," stated Professor E. M. Blaiklock of Auckland University.[2]

"Indeed, taking all the evidence together, it is not too much to say that there is no historic incident better or more variously supported than the resurrection of Christ," wrote Canon Westcott, a Cambridge scholar.[3]

"What gives a special authority to the list [of witnesses] as historical evidence is the reference to most of the five hundred brethren being still alive. St. Paul says, in effect, 'If you do not believe me, you can ask them,'" asserted Dr. Edwin M. Yamauchi, a professor of history at Miami (Ohio) University.[4]

Dr. Paul L. Maier, professor of ancient history at Western Michigan University, stated that "if all the evidence is weighed carefully and fairly, it is indeed justifiable, according to the canons of historical research, to conclude that the tomb in which Jesus was buried was actually empty on the morning of the first Easter. And no shred of evidence has yet been discovered in literary sources, epigraphy or archaeology that would disprove this statement."[5]

Lord Caldecote, lord chief justice of England, has written:

My faith began with and was grounded on what I thought was revealed in the Bible. When, particularly, I came to the New Testament, the Gospels and other writings of the men who had been friends of Jesus Christ seemed to me to make an overwhelming case, merely as a matter of strict evidence, for the fact therein stated . . . The same approach to the cardinal test of the claims of Jesus Christ, namely, His resurrection, has led me, as often as I have tried to examine the evidence, to believe it as fact beyond dispute.

Maier also said,

Where did Christianity first begin? To this the answer must be: "Only one spot on earth—the city of Jerusalem." But this is the very last place it could have started if Jesus' tomb remained occupied, since anyone producing a dead Jesus would have driven a wooden stake through the heart of an incipient Christianity inflamed by His supposed resurrection.

What happened in Jerusalem seven weeks after the first Easter could have taken place only if Jesus' body were somehow missing from Joseph's tomb, for otherwise the Temple establishment, in its imbroglio with the Apostles, would simply have aborted the movement by making a brief trip over to the sepulcher of Joseph of Arimathea and unveiling exhibit A. They did not do this, because they knew the tomb was empty. Their official explanation for it— that the disciples had stolen the body—was an admission that the sepulcher was indeed vacant.

Both Jewish and Roman sources and traditions acknowledge an empty tomb. These sources range from the Jewish historian Josephus to a compilation of fifth-century Jewish writings called the Toledoth Jeshu. Maier called this "positive evidence from a hostile source, which is the strongest kind of historical evidence. In essence, this means that if a source admits a fact decidedly not in its favor, then that fact is genuine."[6]

Both Jewish and Roman sources and traditions acknowledge an empty tomb.

After the close of World War II, Konrad Adenauer, the chancellor of a new Germany, was asked the question: "Do you believe in the resurrection of Jesus Christ?" Adenauer said, "I believe it is the only hope for mankind."

All these testimonies declare: He is alive. Scripture, reason, tradition, prophecy, history, proclamation, sacrament, prayer, and experience—all point to that truth. The resurrection of Jesus Christ is the power of God to change history and to change lives.

The evidence is overwhelming, yet some still doubt. Here are some other witnesses to the Resurrection.

In 1 Corinthians 15:14–58, the apostle Paul argued that because of the Resurrection:

- Our preaching is powerful and significant.

- The words of the apostles can be trusted.

- Our sins are forgiven.

- We have hope of eternal life.

- We are of all humanity the most joyous people.

- We can look to a physical resurrection of our own bodies.

- Death cannot hold our souls.

The greatest news of all is that the Resurrection vindicates forever the mind and heart of God in Christ. We see how the glorious fact of the resurrection of Jesus of Nazareth validates His mission and His message.

The Resurrection shows the victory of the suffering and scandal of the Cross. It is God's self-revelation. It vindicated the prophetic statements of Jesus about His resurrection. He said, "I will rise again." He told those who sought a sign from Him of His deity that the only sign He would give was that of Jonah, signifying that just as Jonah was in the belly of the great fish for three days, so Jesus would be dead in the earth three days.

Because of the Resurrection, certain things are eternally true, and I've noted just a few of them. Death itself was defeated. The persecuted church did not suffer in vain, nor does it today. An entirely new world order with Christ as King was established. Jesus' teachings were ratified. His sacrifice of Himself for our sins was accepted. His suffering achieved His glorious victory. His victory over sin was demonstrated, and His messianic Sonship was declared. His life as fulfillment of the seed of Abraham through the line of King David was made known (Acts 2:29–31; see Ps. 16). His authority was established (Matt. 28:16–20). His deity was demonstrated. His power to live now was shown. His creation was redeemed—as in Adam it was harmed, so in Christ it was made whole.

> *The bodily resurrection of Jesus was followed by the bodily Ascension. He lives today, interceding for His own.*

Please remember, the Resurrection is not a mere concept or symbol. It is living reality. It is real not only in the memories of His disciples, but also in all of His earthly followers to this very day. It is validation of history.

Remember, too, the bodily resurrection of Jesus was followed by the bodily *Ascension*. He lives today, interceding for His own. Oh, what a Savior! And He is coming again to rule and to reign as the living Lord on this earth. It is the greatest news ever uttered. With the hymn writer Alfred H. Ackley, we declare,

He lives. He lives. Christ Jesus lives today!
He walks with me and talks with me along life's narrow way.
He lives. He lives. Salvation to impart!
You ask me how I know He lives: He lives within my heart.

SOME CONVINCING PROOFS

For many years as an agnostic, I doubted the supernatural, especially the biblical claim that Jesus of Nazareth had been raised from the dead. Then, in answer to my saintly mother's prayers, I received Christ, and God gave me good reasons to believe in the Resurrection.

I found we need not be timid where Scripture is bold. The apostle Luke, a medical doctor and certainly the most scientific mind among the disciples, reported that Jesus showed "himself alive after his passion by many infallible proofs, being seen of them forty days, and speaking of the things pertaining to the kingdom of God" (Acts 1:3 KJV).

I am fully convinced that the resurrection of Jesus is the most trustworthy and spectacular event in history. It is like a great mountain peak protruding into the skies, above the clouds, standing out as the most momentous occurrence since creation. Since 1945, I have spent many years studying the Resurrection, including five years as a student at Princeton and Fuller Theological Seminaries, learning from some of the most famous and godly scholars of history. I have come to some definite conclusions that are among the "many infallible proofs" referred to in Acts 1:3 that attest to the authenticity of the Resurrection. Here they are:

1. Jesus predicted His resurrection. Both the prediction and the Resurrection are compelling. Together, they pose a simple question: Shall we believe what Jesus said?

2. The Resurrection is the only reasonable explanation for the empty tomb.

3. The Resurrection is the only reasonable explanation for the early disciples' change from cowering and fearful followers into bold proclaimers of a living Lord.

4. The Resurrection is the only reasonable explanation for the growth of the church in the face of intense and murderous persecution.

5. The Resurrection is the only reasonable explanation for the hundreds of persons who witnessed the resurrected Christ (1 Cor. 15:6).

6. The Resurrection is the only reasonable explanation for the total transformation of Saul of Tarsus from a zealous Pharisee engaged in systematic persecution of Christians to Paul the apostle, who became the most prolific advocate of Christ as resurrected Savior and living Lord.

AND IF HE ROSE . . .

Now, let me ask you a question: What if Jesus *did* rise from the dead? What could it mean to you? Think about it with me.

If He arose, the world can no longer be the same. If He arose, the resurrection of Jesus Christ is the most amazing event in history for all that it discloses. If He arose, God exists. If He arose, He has power over death. If He arose, God loves humanity so much He sent His Son to die for our sins. If He arose, God is a person we can know intimately in our daily experience. If He arose, His promises seem to me to be totally reliable for life today and heaven tomorrow.

It is immensely important to know that Jesus physically, in a body, rose from the dead. The disciples "held his feet" (Matt. 28:9). He seemed to be merely another traveler on the road to Emmaus (Luke 24:15–18, 28–29). He physically took bread and broke it in the presence of others

(Luke 24:30). He ate a piece of broiled fish (Luke 24:42). He appeared, not like a spirit, but as the gardener to Mary (John 20:15). He showed them His hands and His side (John 20:20). Separately, Christ invited the disciple Thomas to reach out and touch His hands and His side (John 20:27). He prepared breakfast for His disciples (John 21:12–13). He plainly stated, "Behold My hands and My feet, that it is I Myself. Handle Me and see, for a spirit does not have flesh and bones as you see I have" (Luke 24:39 NKJV). Peter said that the disciples "ate and drank with him after he rose from the dead" (Acts 10:41).

If He arose, God exists. If He arose, He has power over death. If He arose, God loves humanity so much He sent His Son to die for our sins.

Christianity is not to be compared to other religions because it alone deals with the human body as a matter of eternal consequence. It is crucial that we recall God the Creator, when He made the human body, declared, "It was very good." The truth is that Christ is in a physical body to this day. Stephen saw Christ "standing at the right hand" of the Father in heaven (Acts 7:55–56 NKJV). He will return bodily.

"Those who view spirituality as something related only to a person's inner life are in tragic error," says Dr. Lawrence O. Richards. "It is in our bodily life on earth that sin found expression, and it is in our bodily life on earth with all of its relationships that Christ's gift of newness is also to find expression and in which Jesus is to be revealed."[7] References by the apostle Paul to a "spiritual" body do *not* mean a nonmaterial body. His word in the Greek is *pneumatika* and never means "nonphysical." (Rom. 1:11; 1 Cor. 2:13, 3:1, 14:37; Gal 6:1).

Nevertheless, the body of our Lord was a transformed and glorified body that gives us understanding of the kind of bodies that believers in

Christ will have in heaven: "For our citizenship is in heaven, from which also we eagerly wait for a Savior, the Lord Jesus Christ; who will transform the body of our humble state into conformity with the body of His glory, by the exertion of the power that He has even to subject all things to Himself" (Phil. 3:20–21 NASB).

As the Westminster Confession states regarding "the State of Man After Death, and of the Resurrection of the Dead":

1. The bodies of men, after death, return to dust, and see corruption; but their souls (which neither die nor sleep), having an immortal subsistence, immediately return to God who gave them. The souls of the righteous, being then made perfect in holiness, are received into the highest heavens, where they behold the face of God in light and glory, waiting for the full redemption of their bodies; and the souls of the wicked are cast into hell, where they remain in torments and utter darkness, reserved to the judgment of the great day. Besides these two places for souls separated from their bodies, the Scripture acknowledgeth none.

2. At the last day, such as are found alive shall not die, but be changed; and all the dead shall be raised up with the selfsame bodies, and none other, although with different qualities, which shall be united again to their souls forever.[8]

I find both points true to Scripture and strong pillars to lean on. The empty tomb of our risen Lord encourages and excites me to this very day.

When you are defeated by sin, go to the empty tomb. Perhaps you will see Mary and Martha and Mary Magdalene and many others joyously telling you: "We saw where He had been buried, and the tomb was empty. We told others. They came. We thrilled to the emptiness of that tomb."

When you wonder if your work is in vain, go to the tomb. Look at the awesome line of pilgrims throughout the ages who believed this truth:

> "O death, where is your victory?
>
> O death, where is your sting?"
>
> For sin is the sting that results in death, and the law gives sin its power. How we thank God, who gives us victory over sin and death through Jesus Christ our Lord! So, my dear brothers and sisters, be strong and steady, always enthusiastic about the Lord's work, for you know that nothing you do for the Lord is ever useless. (1 Cor. 15:55–58)

"WHEN I SURVEY THE WONDROUS CROSS"

When I survey the wondrous cross
on which the Prince of glory died,
My richest gain I count but loss,
and pour contempt on all my pride.

Were the whole realm of nature mine,
that were a present far too small;
Love so amazing, so divine,
demands my soul, my life, my all.

—Isaac Watts

THIRTEEN

HOME

Departures are all alike; it is the landfall that crowns the voyage.
—C. S. LEWIS, *LETTERS TO MALCOLM*

On one journey home from Asia, I "really flew." We departed Japan for the customary routing, with a scheduled stopover for fueling in Hawaii, en route to Los Angeles. But about the time I expected to land in Honolulu, the pilot announced we were landing in Los Angeles! We had flown nonstop from Tokyo to LA without stopping for fuel! It meant an early reunion with my family. It was wonderful, but how did it happen?

I chanced to be walking alongside the pilot as we left the airplane. He explained that there was a "super tailwind" in the winds aloft, and by climbing to that level, we experienced the fantastic power of that wind. In fact, he said, we came within two minutes of breaking the world speed record for that crossing.

"Why didn't you step on it?" I joshed.

With no trace of humor, the captain replied, "My first obligation is to the safety and security of our passengers."

I have often thought about that flight and have found a couple of reflections of the truth of God in it. The first is that the Holy Spirit is like that super tailwind, able to propel us forward into achievements for God that we never could imagine in our own strength. The second is that God, like the pilot, is the sovereign Captain of my ship of life. His first priority is my safety and security. I can trust Him never to play games with my life. I can model my own life after His way of dealing responsibly with others. He is a great Father, always looking for ways to bring His children together. He is not a child abuser. He will not let me be mistreated by anyone beyond His care and keeping. And when it comes to the journey to my heavenly home, He knows what timing is best. It truly is fun to fly when God is in control!

All our journeys here on earth are only trails leading to our real home, heaven. Charles Spurgeon once prayed, "May we live here like strangers and make the world not a house, but an inn, in which we sup and lodge, expecting to be on our journey tomorrow."[1] Knowing that heaven is our real home makes it easier to pass through the tough times here on earth. I have taken comfort often in the knowledge that the perils of a journey on earth will be nothing compared to the glories of heaven.

Heaven will be marvelous, and I am excited about going there. I have been reminded of some earthly humorous stories about heaven. I think the Bible supports humor so long as we are not mocking the Lord or His Word. Solomon wrote, "A cheerful heart is good medicine" (Prov. 17:22).

In the hospital recently I heard the story of a couple in their nineties who had been health-food fanatics. They arrived in heaven and found it so joyous, the husband said to the wife: "Honey, if it had not been for you and all those food supplements, we could have been enjoying this wonderful place years ago!"

But, of course, the main joy of heaven will be the heavenly Father greeting us in a time and place of rejoicing, celebration, joy, and great reunion. It will have the dynamics we see in the parable of the prodigal son, returning home from his fallen journey: "So he returned home to his father. And while he was still a long distance away, his father saw him coming. Filled with love and compassion, he ran to his son, embraced him, and kissed him" (Luke 15:20). That may be the only place in holy Scripture where we see God in a hurry—actually running to meet the returning child. So, for followers of Christ, our home is the place where the Father delights in welcoming us even as He sees us coming a long way off. We can expect expressions of love beyond measure; perhaps the intimacy of a hug from God the Father and our Lord Jesus Christ will be our first joy. Wrapped in His loving embrace, we will sense peace, delight, assurance, abundant love, warm fellowship, total security, and absolute calm.

Heaven pulses with such purity and joy that it is impossible for anyone to describe it all. Who am I to try to give words to the creation of His Majesty? One thing I know for sure: heaven itself will reflect the character of our great God. It will be a place of holiness, righteousness, love, justice, mercy, peace, order, and His sovereign rule.

> *One thing I know for sure: heaven itself will reflect the character of our great God.*

"Here we are too prone to think highly of our knowledge," said John Newton, author of "Amazing Grace" and a former slave trader who became a preacher of the gospel. "But when we arrive in yonder world of light, to see Him as He is, we shall be ashamed of the highest conceptions we had of Him, and of our most labored attempts to express them." That fairly well describes my feelings. But proclaim heaven we must.

"It is since Christians have largely ceased to think of the other world that they have become so ineffective in this," said C. S. Lewis in *Mere Christianity*. Then he added in *The Problem of Pain*: "We are very shy nowadays of even mentioning Heaven. We are afraid of the jeer about 'pie in the sky,' and of being told that we are trying to 'escape from the duty of making a happy world here and now into dreams of a happy world elsewhere.' But either there is 'pie in the sky' or there is not. If there is not, then Christianity is false, for this doctrine is woven into its whole fabric. If there is, then this truth, like any other, must be faced, whether it is useful at political meetings or not."

My joyous anticipation of heaven as my home has always been tempered by my realization that not everyone may be there. The other destination of fallen mankind is hell. I was never personally motivated by fear of hell, but I came to realize that I had not given hell the proper emphasis, as did our Lord Jesus. He spoke more of hell than of heaven, and that should be reason enough for His followers to be candid about the awful option. I do not believe God sends people to hell. It is a place, Jesus said, that was created for the devil and his angels. He called it "the eternal fire prepared for the Devil and his demons" (Matt. 25:41). The unforgiven sins of people will send them to hell. As theologian Wayne Grudem puts it, "The devil's characteristic has been to originate sin and tempt others to sin," and that sin, without Christ's saving grace, will cause us to be residents of hell.[2]

Jonathan Edwards, recognized as one of America's greatest scholars and theologians and famous revivalist of the Great Awakening of the eighteenth century, preached about the horrors of hell:

To help your conception, imagine yourself to be cast into a fiery oven, all of a glowing heat, or into the midst of a glowing brick kiln, or of a great furnace, where your pain would be as much greater than that occasioned by accidentally touching a coal of fire, as the heat is greater. Imagine also that your body were to lie there for a quarter of an hour, full of fire, as full within and without as a bright coal of fire, all the while full of quick sense; what horror would you feel at the entrance of such a furnace! And how long would that quarter of an hour seem to you! . . . And how much greater would be the effect, if you knew you must endure it for a whole year, and how vastly greater still, if you knew you must endure it for a thousand years! O then, how would your heart sink, if you thought, if you knew, that you must bear it forever and ever! . . . That after millions of millions of ages, your torment would be no nearer to an end, than ever it was; and that you never, never should be delivered! But your torment in Hell will be immeasurably greater than this illustration represents.[3]

The Bible refers to hell 167 times. But never forget, there is a cross at the entrance to hell. The only way a person can go there is to push the cross aside and deliberately reject God's love and forgiveness. Jesus described the place of final and eternal punishment as the "lake of fire" (Rev. 20:14–15). God did not establish hell for the purpose of scaring people into heaven. Nevertheless, it is a biblical fact that a place of eternal punishment exists, and those who do not know Jesus as their personal Savior ignore it to their own destruction.

I thank God for His salvation through Jesus. I do not see how anyone could come to his dying days and not have his eternal destination settled. If I were unsure about this, there is no way I could have had such joy in these precious closing months of my life. It has been my privilege in these dying days to pray with three nurses, one doctor, and four aides as they prayed receiving Christ as their personal Savior and Lord. How about you? It is time for you to choose whether you want to go to heaven or hell when you die.

Please take this opportunity to settle the question of where you will spend eternity, once and for all. Even if there is a remote possibility that there is a burning hell, do you dare take this chance? What do you possibly have to lose by genuinely receiving Christ and knowing for sure that He has eliminated even the faintest possibility that you could go to hell? My urgent prayer is that you will choose Jesus and heaven, and that you will help countless others make the same precious decision so that they, too, may "live in the house of the LORD forever" (Ps. 23:6).

Prayer is talking with God. Why not talk with Him right now and express your desire to become His child? God knows your heart, and He is not as concerned with your words as He is with the attitude of your heart. The following is a suggested prayer:

Lord Jesus, I need You. I acknowledge that I have sinned against You. Thank You for dying on the cross for my sins and rising from the dead to give me eternal life. I open the door of my heart and receive You as my Savior and

Lord. Take control of the throne of my life. Make me the kind of person You
want me to be.

If you prayed that prayer with a sincere and believing heart, God heard
and answered your prayer. This day you have begun the most exciting, ful-
filling adventure one can ever experience. You have become a part of His
eternal family, and heaven is your home! But this is just the beginning. In
order to experience a bit of heaven here on earth, there are basic truths
you need to know, and you can find them in the Appendix. Please read
them. You can have assurance of your salvation.

THE HEAVENLY SCENE

Holy Scripture is replete with many details of heaven, and Jesus spoke of
it often. So we can know much, if dimly, about our eternal home.

Heaven, I am confident, will not involve a place where we must check
in with Saint Peter, as suggested by many American jokes. Of course, that
cherished Apostle will be one we eventually will want to see and fellowship with. But we are saints with him and he with us (Rom. 1:1)—all of
us sinners who have experienced the grace of our Lord Jesus Christ by
faith alone. For those who know our Savior, our reservations are already
made—bought and paid for by Jesus Himself. There will be no waiting
room or threshold with a pavilion for standing in line as if we were
approaching Disney World. Upon our passing from this earth, our conscious souls are immediately in the presence of our Lord (2 Cor. 5:6). One
moment we are "here," and the next moment we are "there." God is not
the author of any confused reservations system whose computers might
crash and temporarily leave us suspended in limbo (1 Cor. 14:33).

"While your family tends to your funeral, you are beholding the face
of Christ," wrote Erwin W. Lutzer in *One Minute After You Die*. "Though
the family weeps at your departure, you would not return to earth even if
the choice were given to you. Having seen heaven, you will find that earth

has lost all its attraction." This is, in part, why the apostle Paul said for himself it was "far better" to die and go on to be with the Lord in heaven, though he was willing to linger for the benefit of his disciples.

Joni Eareckson Tada, a quadriplegic and mighty woman of God whom I have long admired for her love of our Lord and faithfulness to Him, writes in *Heaven: Your Real Home*:

> I can still hardly believe it. I, with shriveled, bent fingers, atrophied muscles, gnarled knees, and no feeling from the shoulders down, will one day have a new body—light, bright and clothed in righteousness—powerful and dazzling.
>
> Can you imagine the hope this gives someone spinal-cord injured like me? . . . No other religion, no other philosophy promises new bodies, hearts and minds. Only in the gospel of Christ do hurting people find such incredible hope.

Heaven for me, based on the promises of Jesus and the clear descriptions of the Holy Bible, has some other distinctive characteristics.

First, it is a literal and specific place promised and prepared by Jesus for those who follow Him (John 14:1–3). Unless He is a liar—which is unthinkable—He has gone to "prepare a place for you." Two definite aspects make it desirable: it is a place of comfort, and it is where we have a "dwelling" with the Lord God. The King James Version word *mansion* may be both misleading and properly suggestive. It will be a big, beautiful, elegant place, and in that way it may seem like a mansion. Because the modern world has so many physical mansions, we are inclined to respond to that word as if we will live in a sprawling house with an incredible view of a lake and a golf course. But that does heaven a huge disservice. It is so much more because the intensity of the "dwelling" of heaven will be focused on the Main Dweller, the Owner of the specific place, God the Father and Jesus, the Messiah. The comfort Jesus commanded us to think about when we think of heaven suggests the absence of any loneliness ever, the lack of anything fearful, and the presence of totally satisfying assurance in a loving abode. There we will dwell forever.

Further affirmation of a literal heaven is Christ's miraculous ascension into heaven. In Acts 1:9–11 (NASB), two angels flatly told the disciples: "Men of Galilee, why do you stand looking into the sky? This Jesus, who has been taken up from you into heaven, will come in just the same way as you have watched Him go into heaven." Twice the angels declared the fact that Jesus was gone to heaven.

Also, it is a place that lasts for all time and eternity. Heaven is full of purity and special light. Revelation 22:3–5 (NASB) states,

> There shall no longer be any curse; and the throne of God and of the Lamb shall be in it, and His bond-servants will serve Him; and they shall see His face, and His name shall be on their foreheads. And there shall no longer be any night; and they shall not have need of the light of a lamp nor the light of the sun, because the Lord God shall illumine them; and they shall reign forever and ever.

We will have no preoccupation with such details. Our greatest earthly comparison of a regal vacation with everything provided by a billionaire host utterly fails to come close to the complete anticipation of all our needs in heaven.

Paul mentioned he was "caught up into the third heaven" in what appears to have been an out-of-the-body experience that assured him heaven is far above the earth and its atmosphere (2 Cor. 12:2). As a rendezvous, it is a specific place located in the north (Ps. 48:2; Isa. 14:13) where God, the great Lover of eternity, meets His bride-to-be, the church, the congregation of believers, the called-out ones who have responded to the love and mercy of the Father through faith in the finished work of the Son (Heb. 12:22–24).

Out of heaven's registry, the Lamb's Book of Life, we can know our reservations have been recorded so that we may enter—only by the absolute virtue of the blood of the Savior shed on the cross for us and not by any work of righteousness we have done (Luke 10:20; Eph. 2:8–9; Titus 3:5; Rev. 20:11–15). Our DNA would have tested positive in the courts of eternity without the transfusion of His life-giving crimson cure, bought and paid for by Jesus of Nazareth.

In its relief, heaven gives the believer complete escape from the punishment of hell, removes all tears, all pain, all frustration, all mourning, all death (Rev. 21:4). But it is not the mere absence of these displeasures that makes the place heaven.

The features of heaven astound the human mind. Its beauty is "made ready as a bride adorned for her husband" and "having the glory of God" and "like a very costly stone, as a stone of crystal-clear jasper." The foundation stones of the city wall are adorned with "every kind of precious stone." Each of the twelve gates of the city is made of one pearl. The street is of a unique gold, pure and virtually transparent. Flowing from the "throne of God and of the Lamb" is the water of life, crystal clear (Rev. 21–22:1 NASB).

Southern Baptist leader Paige Patterson writes in *Heaven* how the place is gained by faith:

> Somehow Abraham, beginning a long, tedious journey in the troubled Ur of the Chaldees, realized that the city for which he longed would not be of this world. Ur of Abraham's day was a large and beautiful city. Along the way of his sojourn, he passed through other cities of grand design and imperial embellishment. They were all incomplete and imperfect, the habitations of fallen men. Even in Canaan, the Promised Land, there were problems, and Abraham was sometimes one of those problems. Surely, there must be a better place. Therefore, by faith Abraham searched for a city "whose builder and maker is God."

The ultimate place of reward, heaven is where followers of the Messiah of Israel and Savior of the world will have the privilege of giving unto the Lord God all the worship that He alone deserves. In His Sermon on the Mount (Matt. 5:10–12 NKJV), He promised those who suffer for righteousness' sake to stay faithful, "for great is your reward in heaven."

The pilgrim's plunder in heaven, Jesus said, will be for our faith-filled obedience in deciding to "lay up for yourselves treasures in heaven, where neither moth nor rust destroys and where thieves do not break in and steal" (Matt. 6:20 NKJV).

In Luke 12:33 (NASB) Jesus had spoken again of the connection between faithful service on earth and benefits (not salvation, but reward) in heaven: "Sell your possessions and give to charity; make yourselves money belts which do not wear out, an unfailing treasure in heaven, where no thief comes near nor moth destroys." In Revelation 22:12 (NASB) Jesus promised a reward for believers: "I am coming quickly, and My reward is with Me, to render to every man according to what he has done."

But as we reflect on the Lord Jesus and the utter purity of heaven, we will feel unworthy of any recognition. More precisely, we will feel that He and He alone is worthy of honor and attention. As we do, we will place at His feet any crowns of glory we may have earned at the judgment of believers for works done while following Christ in the power of the Holy Spirit (1 Cor. 3:11–15). We will not have in our hands any reward for things done in our own strength or for our own selfish motives (Zech. 4:6).

Believers will receive rewards for doing things in Jesus' name (Matt. 10:42); for being faithful in their service (Luke 19:17); for running the entire race without giving up or giving in (1 Cor. 9:24–25); for cherishing and expecting His Second Coming (2 Tim. 4:7–8); for being faithful in testing (Rev. 2:10); and for all Spirit-led works glorifying God (Rev. 22:12). These other rewards, though of importance, have not been my primary motivation, but I will gladly join in casting any recognitions of me, of any kind, before the feet of our blessed Lord. As I have stated, my primary purpose of ministry to and for our Lord is in response to Him personally: His attributes, His love, His forgiveness, and His offer of life abundant and life eternal.

HOME AT LAST

Enthralled in the presence of the living Lord and Savior, we can expect to engage in the most glorious worship service of all time. No one has any sense of an "order of service." No one is conscious of any worship "style." The Father has set matters in order. The Son is the focus of all eyes. The Spirit prompts the singing of songs. From the lips of sinners saved by amazing grace, from followers of all the ages, come Hosannas to the King of kings and Lord of lords, seated at the right hand of the Father.

The entire angelic host of heaven accompanies the singing of human hearts. Gathered by the stream flowing by the throne of God, the saved of all earth and time come face to face with their Redeemer at last. Each heart lifts in joy just to see Him, to know Him, and to know nothing will ever separate us ever again.

No reunion in history can even foreshadow what joy we will experience as we see loved ones and friends who went on before us. We are known. We are recognized (1 John 3:2). And we identify our loved ones, family, and friends. Brought together in the exquisite, all-surrounding presence of the Lord, our faces beam. Our countenances gleam, and we shout in such delight that angels glance at each other in wonderment: What full-throated, glad-hearted welcomes these blood-washed sinners give each other! How they adore the Lord Jesus! How they love Him! How they love each other!

> *No reunion in history can even foreshadow what joy we will experience as we see loved ones and friends who went on before us.*

Diversity. Jesus "purchased for God with [His] blood men from every tribe and tongue and people and nation . . . a great multitude, which no one could count, from every nation and all tribes and peoples and tongues" (Rev. 5:9; 7:9 NASB). We are Jews and Gentiles, slaves and free, white and black and yellow and red and brown, and male and female. And here there is absolutely no sense of inferiority or superiority. Because we "are complete in Him," there is no sense of prejudice. Unlike most of our Sunday services on earth, we are a vast gathering of peoples from every part of earth, and we realize we are of equal standing in His eyes. We do not admire each other for sensual or physical reasons (Matt. 22:30).

We accept each other because a Mutual Friend in the family, our common Savior, has accepted us. No one's face is veiled, no head covered. We are all of the same caste—the Forgiven Ones, outcast from the worldly, secular, and sensory. We seem to be in a sea of happy faces, a holy, Christ-actualized bliss.

Only partly rendering to Jesus what He eternally deserves, suddenly waves of song go forth. I expect the rejoicing to be unending. Heaven surely will include the spine-tingling sensation of ultimate satisfaction created by the presence of the Lord God Elohim, Jehovah, the Great I Am, Adonai, Messiah. Words cannot form to tell of Him. We cannot conceive of the brilliance of the Savior's appearing. We thought our hearts could believe, but this is far beyond our faith, beyond our dreams, beyond measure. In one word He is *everything*, all in all, now and then and forever. Hallelujah to the Lamb. Reign on, O King eternal. He will fill our senses, our hearts and minds.

Perhaps you can recall the glee of the roller coaster, being tossed in the air by an uncle, the sweet savors of holiday cooking, the aromas of the perfumes of loved ones, the satisfactions of embraces, the security of all bills paid, of all duties done, of all anxieties vanished. That is the least foretaste of heaven, where God-love will be everywhere, in, around, and through us, one to another and to the Father and the Son and the Spirit who makes us one.

With the twenty-four elders we will shout glory to the Lamb slain from the foundation of the earth: "You and You alone are worthy." In Revelation 4:10–11 (NASB), this spontaneous praise is predicted; the twenty-four elders worship Him, saying, "Worthy art Thou, our Lord and our God, to receive glory and honor and power; for Thou didst create all things, and because of Thy will they existed, and were created." Quickly caught up in the praise are the angels of heaven (Rev. 5:11–12 NASB), who declare with a loud voice: "Worthy is the Lamb that was slain to receive power and riches and wisdom and might and honor and glory and blessing."

Next, every living creature will be drawn into praise to the Lord God. Revelation 5:13–14 (NASB) announces that "every created thing which is in heaven and on the earth and under the earth and on the sea, and all things in them, I heard saying, 'To Him who sits on the throne, and to the Lamb, be blessing and honor and glory and dominion forever and ever.'"

Revelation 15:2–4 (NASB) describes those who overcome as they sing in full chorus "the song of the Lamb." The lyrics are specific:

> Great and marvelous are Thy works,
> O Lord God, the Almighty;
> Righteous and true are Thy ways,
> King of the nations!
> Who will not fear, O Lord, and glorify Thy name?
> For Thou alone art holy;
> For all the nations will come and worship before Thee,
> For Thy righteous acts have been revealed.

Jesus will be the focus of all praise. In Revelation 21:23 (NASB) John the apostle recorded that "the city has no need of the sun or of the moon to shine on it, for the glory of God has illumined it, and its lamp is the Lamb."

A REALLY NEW WORLD

In the ultimate renaissance that is heaven, we will feel as fresh as newborn babes, only mature enough to understand this place is so totally different. New, head to toe, heart and mind, soul and body, spirit and strength. There is purity all around, pure air, pure water, pure hearts, crystal-clear minds, righteousness rules; everything is just right. As mighty waters cascading in splendor, righteousness reigns in the courts of our King. There is no—what was that word down there?—there is no sin. Thank You, Lord Jesus. How we were haunted by that old nature—it is gone, too.

We truly will be free at last, totally free, irrevocably set aside in white robes and cleansed consciences, utterly released from all that beset us that short time there upon earth. Free to be who we were meant to be. No more struggle. No more sorrow. No more ill treatment. No abuse. No loss. No unexpected mishap. No momentary breach of fellowship with the Divine Captain of our salvation, the ever-loving Father who seems everywhere hugging us, blessing us, and urging us onward to enjoy all this forever and always. Come, let us adore Him. And we exalt Him. Just as He promised: *nothing* ever separated us from His love, and now and through all the corridors of time, the mountains and valleys, streams and skies of all eternity, we know we will never, ever be separated in any way from Him and each other. Together at last, forever. Amen.

There has never been such a release in all of time to compare to this time of all times. Nothing in our hands we bring. Simply to His cross we cling. No longer the tug of mixed motives. No longer the itch to prevail. No longer the test and the temptation. No more the thought of performing. Gone in full release is all sense of self. We are His, and He is Ours, and We are One with the Father and the Son and the Holy Spirit who makes us One and moves us on in this breathtaking kaleidoscope of joy upon victory upon release upon glory. It not only seems without end; finally, this release, this time, it really is without end. How is it so?

There is only one point of reckoning. It is Jesus: the feet of Jesus, the hands of Jesus, the face of Jesus, the side of Jesus. We know where we are because we see Him and He *knows* us. Some had wondered: Would He say, "Depart from Me. I never knew you"? But we had chosen to trust His promise. We knew He came. He died—see the scars, the nail prints, see His side. Oh, Thomas Didymus. We related to your questioning heart. But we heard Him say: Blessed are those who, having not seen, still believe. And we settled the question. We decided to follow Jesus and place our faith in His finished work of Calvary and the empty tomb, whatever the cost. We believed that even the end of time would find us near "to the dearest and best Who for a world of lost sinners was slain," as the writer of "The Old Rugged Cross" described it.

Because He lives, heaven is home and warmly familiar for each of us. Because the tomb in Jerusalem is *still* empty, we knew we could face all our tomorrows. The light of heaven is powered by His resurrection. We live because He lives. There is no night, no sunset, no dawning. Remember how we would think those sunrises and sunsets were so beautiful? All of them together compose merely a glimpse of the glory and beauty of heaven.

Praise will flow from our hearts. Jesus Christ is Lord. We exalt You, Lord. You are awesome. We love You. We thank You. We fall on our knees and cry, "Holy is the Lord." And for what may seem like a wonderfully long time, we will only be aware of Him, His love, and what He did at Calvary—He died for us. He died for us. He died for us. Amen. Hallelujah to the Lamb of glory.

Dear reader, I look forward to meeting you in God's heaven. Please pray with me:

> *Holy, heavenly Father, thank You for this life and for eternal life. Thank You for the home You have prepared for us in heaven. I pray for those who read this, that Your Holy Spirit will speak to them, and that they may say yes to the Lord Jesus and His completed work of paying for the forgiveness of our sins. May they exchange their lives for Yours and seek to follow Jesus all their days, led by Your Spirit and guided by Your Word, until we all stand before You in the glad and glorious eternal light of heaven. In Jesus' name, I pray and praise You. Amen!*

Because the tomb in Jerusalem is still empty, we knew we could face all our tomorrows.

Epilogue

*O*ur God is awesome, and He confounds the wisdom of this world. He uses individuals to accomplish His holy purposes throughout the earth. If He can use a young couple from Oklahoma to help reach the world with the good news of our Creator God and Savior, Jesus Christ, then He can use you. In your youth. In your strength. In the declining years. In the throes of pain and suffering. In the seeming despair of the shadow of death. He can use you to pray, to enjoy His presence, to envision great things for Him and do what you can to move His kingdom's work along, day by day, in your life, home, community and in that share of global reach with which you connect.

Vonette and I have experienced so many mountaintop events—our marriage, the arrival of our sons, later their wives and children, the contract with Jesus and the vision of Campus Crusade for Christ, watching billions of copies of the Four Spiritual Laws and its descendants go around the world, the creation of the *JESUS* film and its viewing by more than 5.5 billion persons in more than 800 languages in 235 countries and provinces. Numerous campaigns like Explo '72, Explo '74, Explo '85, "I Found It," "Here's Life World," and the "Discover God" movement. And the birth of each of more than 70 ministries within Campus Crusade is of equal significance.

But since these dying days have come upon me, God has given me some of the most exciting work of my life to do. I received a telephone call from Dr. James O. Davis, a well-known evangelist with a worldwide ministry. He was burdened for pastors everywhere. My heart has always been with pastors. Spirit-filled pastors who preach and teach God's Word and exalt Christ are the most strategic people in any community. Spirit-filled members go forth into their communities as salt and light. They need our prayers and support. So God gave us a vision of developing and deploying a Global Pastors Network to help plant 5 million house churches and encourage millions of existing pastors across the globe and equip them to help fulfill the Great Commission. It has been thrilling to watch God unfold this plan.

> *Don't look at the clock or the calendar, but look upon our all-powerful God.*

I report all this amid hospitals and doctors and physical restrictions to the praise and glory of our faithful God and to encourage you: listen for God's ideas and ask Him to show you how to implement them. Don't look at the clock or the calendar, but look upon our all-powerful God: "Now glory be to God! By his mighty power at work within us, he is able to accomplish infinitely more than we would ever dare to ask or hope" (Eph. 3:20).

None of us has a long time here on planet Earth. It is like a staging ground. It is our split second in eternity when we have an opportunity to invest our lives, our time, our talent and our treasure to help fulfill what our Lord came into this world to do and commissioned us to do. In fact, His last command before He ascended to be with the Father was: "Be my witnesses."

My eye of faith can see just beyond the sunset to my home in the glorious presence of our matchless Creator-God and Savior, the Lord Jesus Christ. Soon, it will all be right. Thank you for taking part of the journey with me.

*M*y personal journey with my husband, right up to his coronation, filled me with a great sense of how loving, considerate, thoughtful, and awesome our God really is. The Lord never failed Bill or me one time from the moment we heard the news of "terminal illness" right through his passing and his body's burial. God has continued to sustain me and bless me in ways I never expected and from thousands of expressions pouring upon me like a refreshing waterfall. My lips simply must speak and sing of our Lord's faithfulness and goodness to us both. We enjoyed fifty-four years, seven months, and twenty days of marriage that were rich and rewarding, and when the time came for Bill to go to be with Jesus, we both knew it.

I do want to praise God for three miracles— *where* Bill passed away, *when,* and especially *how* he went to be with the Lord. In 2000 when the doctors announced Bill's life soon would be taken, I joined him in praying for both a miracle of healing and/or supernatural grace in dying. I personally prayed for a miracle of healing and was blessed with how many new initiatives in treating and perhaps curing pulmonary fibrosis came into our lives in three years' time. After Bill had a painful biopsy taken in Colorado in November, we went to Arrowhead Springs. We enjoyed several weeks of fellowship with our son Zac's family. Then in March 2001 Bill

> *I do want to praise God for . . . where Bill passed away, when, and especially how he went to be with the Lord.*

decided, "I would rather go home on a plane than be shipped home in a box," and we returned to our Orlando home the weekend of Easter 2001. There is no doubt that being home helped. For the balance of 2001 and all of 2002, Bill was able to work at an amazing pace. One aide counted 80 projects he was working on at once—including books, booklets, scripts, videos, and CDs. In early 2003 we accepted hospice care and their thoughtful suggestions. Bill, though he was hospitalized several times, did not want to die in a hospital or treatment facility; he wanted to be home. God orchestrated that, making matters much easier for family and friends and staff. It helped a lot to be home.

I still rejoice in the timing of Bill's passing, coming as it did, amid the staff training conference, which only occurs every two years. Although it made some matters hectic, it really enabled our extended family to join in the experience and celebration, to facilitate grieving and to bless our own family in tremendous ways. God used it to clarify to me that I was to keep serving and not be focused on the loss and myself. Afterward, someone mentioned the example of Ezekiel: "and in the evening my wife died. The next morning I did everything I had been told to do"—despite what social customs and religious rituals of the time required (Ezek. 24:18).

As recorded earlier in this book, I took great refuge in God's sovereignty in Bill's dying days from the passage in John 14:28: "If you really love me, you will be very happy for me, because now I can go to the Father, who is greater than I am."

A HIGHER AUTHORITY

Let me unfold the miracle of *how* he left this world. The doctors had said his death would be filled with the anguish of suffocation. I respect and have high regard for those doctors. They predicted with the knowledge of humanity. But God has the last word on the death of His saints, and He certainly overruled as Bill passed without the awful struggle that had been predicted. "Precious in the sight of the Lord is the death of his saints," says the Scripture (Ps. 116:15 NIV), and so it was for Bill.

About ten days before he passed, while he was quite lucid, Bill beckoned our son Brad into his room and asked for a specific time of prayer. Bill had read of the last words of both saints and sinners. It had bothered him that some Christians of great repute had used curse words in their final hours. Sometimes under the stress of dying pain or under medications, their words did not bring glory to our God. Bill could not tolerate the thought that his lips in his last hours might somehow bring reproach to the name of our Lord Jesus. He and Brad prayed together, urging God to take his life before his lips uttered anything but praise for our Lord. God granted him that request.

One of the most moving moments of all came on a Friday, July 11, as Steve Douglass, president of Campus Crusade for Christ, telephoned from San Diego, where he was meeting with the international directors and leaders of Campus Crusade. Each of these leaders came to the phone and brought greetings and a word of encouraging news about ministry projects all over the world. Thousands were coming to Christ on every continent. They had prepared and signed a paper pledging their lives to carry out the vision God had given Bill to help fulfill the Great Commission every year until our Lord returns. They promised Bill's work would go on. Then they faxed a document with these words:

Dearest Bill & Vonette,

Thank you for your exemplary leadership for over 50 years.

We hereby confirm in writing our commitment with you over the telephone on July 7, 2003:

So long as the Lord gives us breath we will, through the power of the Holy Spirit, walk in the love of Jesus Christ.

From this foundation we will do our part to help fulfill the Great Commission by:

- *Boldly proclaiming Jesus Christ*
- *Developing leaders*
- *Mobilizing partners and co-laborers*
- *Helping reach every person everywhere until the Lord returns*

Together, then, we commit to help build movements everywhere, so that everyone knows someone who truly follows Jesus.

It was signed by forty-one leaders from many nations. My heart was so full, I dropped to my knees at Bill's bedside, and we wept tears of joy and gratitude. We thanked our wonderful God for this tremendous assurance that God would continue what He had begun in Bill. It was awesome!

Bill began to lose ground physically the nearer we came to the date of the Christian Booksellers Association (CBA) convention, which was held near our Orlando home. On the day of the Sister Circle Tea (July 11) for women representatives of publishers, a neighbor volunteered to have the tea in her home. Bill showed the first serious signs that he was not going to recover. He insisted I attend the Tea. It was beautiful. I think the women were ministered to, as I received sweet notes from most of them. Though mentally alert, Bill was having difficulty making himself understood in his speech.

Saturday, July 12, he had trouble dictating his last project, "A Charge to the Staff." We tried to interpret for him and I think achieved his purpose. It meant much to him to exhort and encourage the staff (and all followers of Jesus) with his last productive breaths. With the nurse and I alternately leaning near his face, he dictated the charge, and we had it quickly processed for presentation. His charge was entitled "Following Jesus of Nazareth" and here it is:

FOLLOWING JESUS OF NAZARETH

Beloved followers of Christ around the world, I embrace you with the love of our risen Savior in Whom dwells all the fullness of the Godhead bodily, and through Whom alone we can know our Awesome Creator; now by His Holy Spirit I give you this charge to keep:

Love the Lord God with all your heart,
mind, soul and strength; keep His command-
ments and practice His Golden Rule.

Surrender to our Matchless Master as a royal
slave, obeying and enjoying life with Him,
trusting in His presence, power, and promises.

Meditate upon the attributes of the One True
Living God, and let your faith reflect His
greatness and character in all your ways.

Love your family as Christ loves you.

Depend upon the power of the Holy Spirit
both to begin and to complete His plan for
your role in helping to fulfill the Great
Commission.

Memorize His Holy Word to fortify yourself
for spiritual warfare.

By faith, walk in His light, enjoy His pres-
ence, love with His love, and rejoice that you
are never alone; He is with you, always, to
bless!

He signed it: "*Bill Bright,* Founder, Chairman/President Emeritus, Campus Crusade for Christ," and he wanted it printed on a card with the following Scriptures on the back:

The Great Commandments

Jesus speaking: "Love the Lord your God with all your heart, all your soul, and all your mind . . . Love your neighbor as yourself." (Matt. 22:37–39)

The Golden Rule

Jesus speaking: "Do for others what you would like them to do for you." (Matt. 7:12)

The Ten Commandments

1. "Do not worship any other gods besides me."
2. "Do not make idols of any kind, whether in the shape of birds or animals or fish."
3. "Do not misuse the name of the LORD your God."
4. "Remember to observe the Sabbath day by keeping it holy."
5. "Honor your father and mother."
6. "Do not murder."
7. "Do not commit adultery."
8. "Do not steal."
9. "Do not testify falsely against your neighbor."
10. "Do not covet." (Exod. 20:3–17)

That same day, July 12, he signed his last letters. By Monday, July 14, he did not want me away from his side very long at a time. By Wednesday night, he had almost stopped eating. He was alert enough that day to have a brief meeting with men to discuss a unique film on the person of Jesus. He had prayer for the man and his assistant to ask God's anointing on the project. (In late May, President George W. Bush had called Bill to encourage him. Former President George H. W. Bush also called during the last few days of his life. Many Christian leaders called in the last couple of months.)

The final week doctors ordered a new kind of oxygen mask over Bill's mouth and nose, which made understanding his speech more difficult.

Thursday, July 17, he knew what was going on, but he could no longer communicate. He rarely opened his eyes. But he showed no signs of pain! I started spending time in his bed. He tried unsuccessfully to speak the last time. He seemed resigned to that. He laid his head over on my shoulder. I held his hand most of the time as I had done each night, all night that week. Friday, July 18, I was to speak to the staff in Colorado by Internet. Part of my message was Bill's "Final Charge" on the subject of following our Lord. Bill had suggested I wear red for his memorial service, so for the Internet presentation I decided to wear a red pantsuit with pearls he had given me. I had hesitated over the color but thought by then that red might cheer him up. He seemed to know what was going on but responded little. I'm not sure he saw me in red, but I believe he knew I was wearing it and that I was speaking to staff.

I seldom left his side that day or the next. On Friday afternoon his breathing definitely changed. His vital signs were good (blood pressure 130 over 70) in the morning, and I was told he could last for days. Saturday morning, Steve Douglass, in a telephone conversation, communicated that he wanted me to come to Colorado State University for a memorial service for Bill when he passed away, even if it meant staff would be held over a day. Bill had been scheduled to speak to staff Monday night by video, if he was not able to do so by Internet. I alerted Brad and Katherine to prepare to leave on short notice.

For several previous days, Bill's breathing had been at the pace of forty-four breaths per minute as his body was hungry for oxygen it could not absorb. He pleaded for more oxygen. Some medical attendants were urging that strong sedatives be used. Bill and I had previously discussed this issue, and he had decided he did not want such strong sedatives until absolutely necessary. I told the medical advisers: "This man has too much to offer the world to merely be put out of his misery." He wanted to remain lucid until he had finished all of his projects. Bill's breathing slowed dramatically, to about nineteen breaths per minute. I believe we were told "average" human breathing is about twelve times per minute.

Bailey and Elizabeth Marks had been with us all week beginning Sunday of the week before; Nancy DeMoss had come on Saturday and stayed until Friday; and Barbara and Howard Ball were with us most days of those two weeks.

At 7:00 P.M. Bill's breathing had slowed to eleven breaths a minute and was continuing to drop. It appeared his departure would not be far away.

Mary Jane Morgan had been arranging food to be brought in for dinner each evening. We had eight to ten people for dinner most evenings. That evening Mary Jane, Nina Locke, Ann Drexel, Bailey and Elizabeth Marks, Brad and Katherine with children, Mary Johnston, Donna Sites, and Barbara and Howard Ball, who had come to help that evening. I called them all in to begin to sing hymns around Bill's bed. We had intermittently been singing for him at his request for the previous two or three weeks. He had chosen some of his favorite hymns from Robert Morgan's book *Then Sings My Soul*, which someone had sent to him. I finally recalled the title of a favorite he wanted to hear: "His Name Is Wonderful." Katherine led us in singing and sang to him alone on several occasions.

Bill kept his head turned to the right most of the time. That was the side where I lay beside him with the head of the bed raised, as he liked to sleep most of the time. He had the slightest tinge of a smile on the right side of his mouth and looked very contented and restful. He had praised God in words often until he no longer could move his lips. In those last days and weeks, I had observed something of a pattern: When it seemed he experienced pain, he would stop whatever he was doing—even in midsentence—and say: "Praise you, Father . . . praise, praise, praise." My observation and that of others was that he literally was choosing to turn pain into praise. It was so precious to behold.

We talked to him and read Scripture to him as long as he seemed to listen. Howard Ball read the twenty-third Psalm. Bailey Marks read to him. We covered John 14 and 15, and my last reading to him on Saturday was 1 Corinthians 13, one of his favorite chapters. The footnotes in the *Life Application Bible* spoke to me very clearly.

When Bill's breaths became four and a half per minute, we knew it would not be long before his departure. His brow was smooth, with no sign of stress. He had had no medication since early Thursday morning (no sedatives). He was at peace, but his breathing was labored.

I had expressed my love for him. We had previously discussed the stage of "final moments." I had already made it clear to him that he had my permission to go to heaven anytime he and the Lord determined. We had been advised that this was an important message to convey, and it had already been done.

"My precious angel" became my most frequently used name for him as I had cared for him in the last weeks. Each time I came in the bedroom, while he was lucid, he would greet me with one of his superlatives: "My love, my love, my angel, lover, partner and friend; you are beautiful to behold." How he would carry on.

During our last evening together, he could not speak. He was aware of my presence and what was going on. I felt led to say to him late that final Saturday evening, "I want you to go be with Jesus; you want to go be with Jesus, and Jesus wants you to come to him. Why don't you let him carry you to heaven?" I looked away a moment and looked back expecting the next breath. It did not come. I saw the last sign of heartbeat in his neck. He was gone. We were in the midst of singing as Bill slipped away. It was, as Bailey recalls, exactly 9:25 P.M. EST.

> "*I* want you to go be with Jesus; you want to go be with Jesus, and Jesus wants you to come to him. Why don't you let him carry you to heaven?"

Donna Sites, who came as a nurse that night, said she had seen many people die. Upon entering a patient's room, she said she had always sensed death. Not so with Bill Bright, she said. "I feel only peace and love here," she told us. Bill simply took his last breath on earth and his first breath in heaven. It was as if he had merely transferred his occupancy. Later, I thought of the phrase in the prayer of St. Francis of Assisi: "For it is in dying, we are born to eternal life."

I called Zac and Terry, and while on the phone, we prayed and all sang "How Great Thou Art." We were able to make arrangements to leave for the staff conference in Colorado at noon the next day.

No one rushed around as Bill went to heaven. We lingered, continued to sing around his bedside, prayed, and encouraged each other for nearly an hour before we called the funeral home.

I shall never forget how God used family and friends to support us those last weeks and days and hours. Each face reflected to me God's presence, our common confidence in our great God, and the celebration of all that God had done in and through Bill. We reminisced and rejoiced and again reminisced and rejoiced and fairly shouted each time we realized Bill was with our wonderful Lord, in glorious peace at last, gone from the struggles of this earthly form and present with God—breathing celestial air, no impurities, no disease, no pain, only joy and radiance and peace with our great Creator and Savior and Master.

Both the Colorado service and the formal memorial service in Orlando have been recorded and are still viewable at www.bill.bright@ccci.org. The staff memorial service took place on Monday night, which was the night Bill was scheduled to speak. The formal memorial service, attended by approximately 5,000 persons, was Tuesday, July 30.

Although I have tried to complete as much correspondence as possible, I shall never be able to express my deep gratitude to the thousands of wonderful expressions of love for Bill and for me. So many testified of his influence in their lives as to love, faith, and the power of the Holy Spirit. Their lives stand as a tremendous testimony to our Lord and are a part of his legacy.

Favored by God to have shared his life and
ministry, I am . . .

Vonette Zachary Bright
September 2003
Orlando

ALMOST HOME

"What! almost home?" "Yes, almost home," she said.
And light seemed gleaming on her aged head.
"Jesus is very precious!" Those who near
Her bedside stood were thrilled those words to hear.
"Toward His blest home I turn my willing feet;
Hinder me not; I go my Lord to meet."
Silence ensued. She seemed to pass away,
Serene and quiet as that summer day.
"Speak," cried through tears her daughter, bending low,
"One word, beloved mother, ere you go."
She spoke that word; the last she spoke on earth,
In whispering tones—that word of wondrous worth:
"JESUS!" The sorrowing listeners caught the sound,
But angels heard it with a joy profound.
Back, at its mighty power, the gates unfold—
The gates of pearl that guard the streets of gold.
The harpers with their harps took up the strain,
And sang the triumph of the Lord again,
As through the open portals entered in
Another soul redeemed from death and sin.
And as from earth the spirit passed away,
To dwell forever in the realms of day,
Those who were left to mourn could almost hear
The strains of heavenly music strike the ear.
And to their longing eyes by grace was given,
In such a scene, as 'twere, a glimpse of heaven.

—Anonymous

WOULD YOU LIKE TO KNOW GOD PERSONALLY?

*T*he following four principles will help you discover how to know God personally and experience the abundant life He promised.

1. God **loves** you and created you to know Him personally.

God's Love

"God so loved the world that He gave His one and only Son, that whoever believes in Him shall not perish but have eternal life" (John 3:16 NIV).

God's Plan

"Now this is eternal life: that they may know you, the only true God, and Jesus Christ, whom you have sent" (John 17:3 NIV).

What prevents us from knowing God personally?

2. Man is **sinful** and **separated** from God, so we cannot know Him personally or experience His love.

Man Is Sinful

"All have sinned and fall short of the glory of God" (Romans 3:23 NIV).

Man was created to have fellowship with God; but, because of his own stubborn self-will, he chose to go his own independent way and fellowship with God was broken. This self-will, characterized by an attitude of active rebellion or passive indifference, is an evidence of what the Bible calls sin.

Man Is Separated

"The wages of sin is death" [spiritual separation from God] (Romans 6:23 NIV).

This diagram illustrates that God is holy and man is sinful. A great gulf separates the two. The arrows illustrate that man is continually trying to reach God and the abundant life through his own efforts, such as a good life, philosophy, or religion—but he inevitably fails.

The third principle explains the only way to bridge this gulf . . .

3. Jesus Christ is God's only provision for man's sin. Through Him alone we can know God personally and experience God's love.

He Died in Our Place

"God demonstrates His own love toward us, in that while we were yet sinners, Christ died for us" (Romans 5:8 NKJV).

He Rose from the Dead

"Christ died for our sins . . . He was buried . . . He was raised on the third day according to the Scriptures . . . He appeared to Peter, then to the twelve. After that He appeared to more than five hundred . . ." (1 Corinthians 15:3–6).

He Is the Only Way to God

"Jesus told him, 'I am the way, the truth, and the life. No one can come to the Father, except through Me'" (John 14:6).

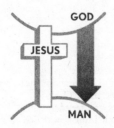

This diagram illustrates that God has bridged the gulf that separates us from Him by sending His Son, Jesus Christ, to die on the cross in our place to pay the penalty for our sins.

It is not enough just to know these three truths . . .

4. *We must individually receive Jesus Christ as Savior and Lord; then we can know God personally and experience His love.*

We Must Receive Christ

"As many as received Him, to them He gave the right to become children of God, to those who believe in His name" (John 1:12 NKJV).

We Receive Christ Through Faith

"For by grace you have been saved through faith, and that not of yourselves; it is the gift of God, not as a result of works, lest anyone should boast" (Ephesians 2:8–9 NKJV).

When We Receive Christ, We Experience a New Birth

(Read John 3:1–8.)

We Receive Christ Through Personal Invitation

[Christ speaking] "Behold, I stand at the door and knock. If anyone hears My voice and opens the door, I will come in to him" (Revelation 3:20).

Receiving Christ involves turning to God from self (repentance) and trusting Christ to come into our lives to forgive our sins and to make us what He wants us to be. Just to agree intellectually that Jesus Christ is the Son of God and that He died on the cross for our sins is not enough. Nor is it enough to have an emotional experience. We receive Jesus Christ by faith, as an act of the will.

These two circles represent two kinds of lives:

Self-Directed Life
S – Self is on the throne
† – Christ is outside the life
● – Interests are directed by self, often resulting in discord and frustration

Christ-Directed Life
† – Christ is in the life and on the throne
S – Self is yielding to Christ
● – Interests are directed by Christ, resulting in harmony with God's plan

Which circle best represents your life?

Which circle would you like to have represent your life?

The following explains how you can receive Christ:

You Can Receive Christ Right Now by Faith Through Prayer (Prayer is Talking with God)

God knows your heart and is not so concerned with your words as He is with the attitude of your heart. The following is a suggested prayer:

> *Lord Jesus, I want to know You personally. Thank You for dying on the cross for my sins. I open the door of my life and receive You as my Savior and Lord. Thank You for forgiving my sins and giving me eternal life. Take control of the throne of my life. Make me the kind of person You want me to be.*

Does this prayer express the desire of your heart? If it does, I invite you to pray this prayer right now, and Christ will come into your life, as He promised.

How to Know That Christ Is in Your Life

Did you receive Christ into your life? According to His promise in Revelation 3:20, where is Christ right now in relation to you? Christ said that He would come into your life and be your friend so you can know Him personally. Would He mislead you? On what authority do you know that God has answered your prayer? (The trustworthiness of God Himself and His Word.)

The Bible Promises Eternal Life to All Who Receive Christ

"God has given us eternal life, and this life is in His Son. He who has the Son has life; he who does not have the Son of God does not have the life" (1 John 5:11–12 NIV).

Thank God often that Christ is in your life and that He will never leave you (Hebrews 13:5). You can know on the basis of His promise that Christ lives in you and that you have eternal life from the very moment you invite Him in. He will not deceive you.

An important reminder . . .

Do Not Depend on Feelings

The promise of God's Word, the Bible—not our feelings—is our authority. The Christian lives by faith (trust) in the trustworthiness of God Himself and His Word. This train diagram illustrates the relationship among fact (God and His Word), faith (our trust in God and His Word), and feeling (the result of our faith and obedience). (Read John 14:21.)

The train will run with or without the caboose. However, it would be useless to attempt to pull the train by the caboose. In the same way, as Christians we do not depend on feelings or emotions, but we place our faith (trust) in the trustworthiness of God and the promises of His Word.

Now That You Have Entered Into a Personal Relationship with Christ

The moment you received Christ by faith, as an act of the will, many things happened, including the following:

- Christ came into your life (Revelation 3:20; Colossians 1:27).
- Your sins were forgiven (Colossians 1:14).
- You became a child of God (John 1:12).
- You received eternal life (John 5:24).
- You began the great adventure for which God created you (John 10:10).

Can you think of anything more wonderful that could happen to you than entering into a personal relationship with Jesus Christ? Would you like to thank God in prayer right now for what He has done for you? By thanking God, you demonstrate your faith.

To enjoy your new relationship with God . . .

Suggestions for Christian Growth

Spiritual growth results from trusting Jesus Christ. A life of faith will enable you to trust God increasingly with every detail of your life, and to practice the following:

G *Go* to God in prayer daily (John 15:7).

R *Read* God's Word daily (Acts 17:11); begin with the Gospel of John.

O *Obey* God moment by moment (John 14:21).

W *Witness* for Christ by your life and words (Matthew 4:19; John 15:8).

T *Trust* God for every detail of your life (1 Peter 5:7).

H *Holy Spirit*—allow Him to control and empower your daily life and witness (Galatians 5:16–17; Acts 1:8; Ephesians 5:18).

Fellowship in a Good Church

God's Word instructs us not to forsake "the assembling of ourselves together" (Hebrews 10:25 NKJV). If you do not belong to a church, do not wait to be invited. Take the initiative; call the pastor of a nearby church where Christ is honored and His Word is preached. Start this week with plans to attend regularly.

SATISFIED?

*W*hat words would you use to describe your current experience as a Christian?

Growing	Frustrated
Disappointing	Fulfilled
Forgiven	Stuck
Struggling	Joyful
Defeated	Exciting
Up and down	Empty
Discouraged	Duty
Intimate	Mediocre
Painful	Dynamic
Guilty	Vital
So-so	Others?

Do you desire more? Jesus said, "If anyone is thirsty, let him come to me and drink. Whoever believes in me, as the Scripture has said, streams of living water will flow from within him" (John 7:37–38 NIV).

What did Jesus mean? John, the biblical author, went on to explain, "By this he meant the Spirit, whom those who believed in him were later to receive. Up to that time the Spirit had not been given, since Jesus had not yet been glorified" (John 7:39 NIV).

Jesus promised that God's Holy Spirit would satisfy the thirst, or deepest longings, of all who believe in Jesus Christ. However, many Christians do not understand the Holy Spirit or how to experience Him in their daily lives.

The following principles will help you understand and enjoy God's Spirit.

THE DIVINE GIFT

Divine: (adj.) given by God

God has given us His Spirit so that we can experience intimacy with Him and enjoy all He has for us.

The Holy Spirit is the source of our deepest satisfaction.

The Holy Spirit is God's permanent presence with us.

Jesus said, "I will ask the Father, and he will give you another Counselor to be with you forever—the Spirit of truth" (John 14:16–17 NIV).

The Holy Spirit enables us to understand and experience all God has given us.

"We have not received the spirit of the world but the Spirit who is from God, that we may understand what God has freely given us" (1 Corinthians 2:12).

The Holy Spirit enables us to experience many things:

- A genuine new spiritual life (John 3:1–8).
- The assurance of being a child of God (Romans 8:15–16).
- The infinite love of God (Romans 5:5; Ephesians 3:18–19).

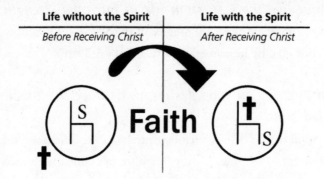

"The man without the Spirit does not accept the things that come from the Spirit of God, for they are foolishness to him, and he cannot understand them, because they are spiritually discerned" (1 Corinthians 2:14 NIV).

"The spiritual man makes judgments about all things . . . We have the mind of Christ" (1 Corinthians 2:15–16 NIV).

"But those who are controlled by the Holy Spirit think about things that please the Spirit" (Romans 8:5).

Why are many Christians not satisfied in their experience with God?

THE PRESENT DANGER
Danger: (n.) a thing that may cause injury, loss, or pain
We cannot experience intimacy with God and enjoy all He has for us if we fail to depend on His Spirit.

People who trust in their own efforts and strength to live the Christian life will experience failure and frustration, as will those who live to please themselves rather than God.

We cannot live the Christian life in our own strength.

"Are you so foolish? After beginning with the Spirit, are you now trying to attain your goal by human effort?" (Galatians 3:3 NIV).

We cannot enjoy all God desires for us if we live by our self-centered desires.

"For the sinful nature desires what is contrary to the Spirit, and the Spirit what is contrary to the sinful nature. They are in conflict with each other, so that you do not do what you want" (Galatians 5:17 NIV).

Three Kinds of Lifestyles

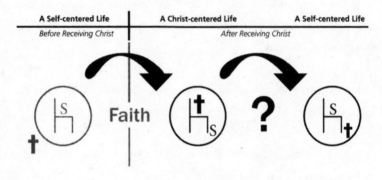

"Brothers, I could not address you as spiritual but as worldly—mere infants in Christ. I gave you milk, not solid food, for you were not yet ready for it. Indeed, you are still not ready. You are still worldly. For since there is jealousy and quarreling among you, are you not worldly? Are you not acting like mere men?" (1 Corinthians 3:1–3 NIV).

How can we develop a lifestyle of depending on the Spirit?

THE INTIMATE JOURNEY

Journey: (n.) any course from one experience to another

By walking in the Spirit we increasingly experience
intimacy with God and enjoy all He has for us.

Walking in the Spirit moment by moment is a lifestyle. It is learning to depend upon the Holy Spirit for His abundant resources as a way of life.

As we walk in the Spirit, we have the ability to live a life pleasing to God.

"So I say, live by the Spirit, and you will not gratify the desires of the sinful nature . . . Since we live by the Spirit, let us keep in step with the Spirit" (Galatians 5:16, 25 NIV).

As we walk in the Spirit, we experience intimacy with God and all He has for us.

"But the fruit of the Spirit is love, joy, peace, patience, kindness, goodness, faithfulness, gentleness and self-control" (Galatians 5:22–23 NIV).

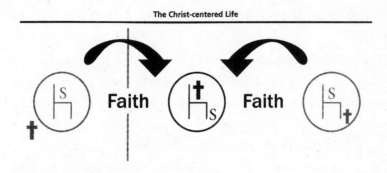

The Christ-centered Life

Faith   Faith

Faith (trust in God and His promises) is the only way a Christian can live by the Spirit.

Spiritual breathing is a powerful word picture which can help you experience moment-by-moment dependence upon the Spirit.

Exhale: Confess your sin the moment you become aware of it—agree with God concerning it and thank Him for His forgiveness, according to 1 John 1:9 and Hebrews 10:1–25. Confession requires repentance—a change in attitude and action.

Inhale: Surrender control of your life to Christ, and rely upon the Holy Spirit to fill you with His presence and power by faith, according to His command (Ephesians 5:18) and promise (1 John 5:14–15).

How does the Holy Spirit fill us with His power?

THE EMPOWERING PRESENCE

Empower: (v.) to give ability to

We are filled with the Spirit by faith, enabling us to experience intimacy with God and enjoy all He has for us.

The essence of the Christian life is what God does in and through us, not what we do for God. Christ's life is reproduced in the believer by the power of the Holy Spirit. To be filled with the Spirit is to be directed and empowered by Him.

By faith, we experience God's power through the Holy Spirit.

"I pray that out of his glorious riches he may strengthen you with power through his Spirit in your inner being, so that Christ may dwell in your hearts through faith" (Ephesians 3:16–17 NIV).

Three important questions to ask yourself:

1. Am I ready now to surrender control of my life to our Lord Jesus Christ? (Romans 12:1–2).
2. Am I ready now to confess my sins? (1 John 1:9). Sin grieves God's Spirit (Ephesians 4:30). But God in His love has forgiven all of your sins—past, present, and future—because Christ has died for you.

3. Do I sincerely desire to be directed and empowered by the Holy Spirit? (John 7:37–39).

By faith claim the fullness of the Spirit according to His command and promise:

God COMMANDS us to be filled with the Spirit.

". . . be filled with the Spirit" (Ephesians 5:18 NIV).

God PROMISES He will always answer when we pray according to His will.

"This is the confidence we have in approaching God: that if we ask anything according to his will, he hears us. And if we know that he hears us—whatever we ask—we know that we have what we asked of him" (1 John 5:14–15).

How to pray to be filled with the Holy Spirit . . .

THE TURNING POINT

Turning point: time when a decisive change occurs
We are filled with the Holy Spirit by faith alone.

Sincere prayer is one way of expressing our faith. The following is a suggested prayer:

Dear Father, I need You. I acknowledge that I have sinned against You by directing my own life. I thank You that You have forgiven my sins through Christ's death on the cross for me. I now invite Christ to again take His place on the throne of my life. Fill me with the Holy Spirit as You commanded me to be filled, and as You promised in Your Word that You would do if I asked in faith. I pray this in the name of Jesus. I now thank You for filling me with the Holy Spirit and directing my life.

Does this prayer express the desire of your heart? If so, you can pray right now and trust God to fill you with His Holy Spirit.

How to know that you are filled by the Holy Spirit

- Did you ask God to fill you with the Holy Spirit?

- Do you know that you are now filled with the Holy Spirit?

- On what authority? (On the trustworthiness of God Himself and His Word: Hebrews 11:6; Romans 14:22–23.)

As you continue to depend on God's Spirit moment by moment, you will experience and enjoy intimacy with God and all He has for you—a truly rich and satisfying life.

An important reminder . . .

Do Not Depend on Feelings

The promise of God's Word, the Bible—not our feelings—is our authority. The Christian lives by faith (trust) in the trustworthiness of God Himself and His Word. Flying in an airplane can illustrate the relationship among fact (God and His Word), faith (our trust in God and His Word), and feeling (the result of our faith and obedience) (John 14:21).

To be transported by an airplane, we must place our faith in the trustworthiness of the aircraft and the pilot who flies it. Our feelings of confidence or fear do not affect the ability of the airplane to transport us, though they do affect how much we enjoy the trip. In the same way we as Christians do not depend on feelings or emotions, but we place our faith (trust) in the trustworthiness of God and the promises of His Word.

Now That You Are Filled with the Holy Spirit

Thank God that the Spirit will enable you:

- to glorify Christ with your life (John 16:14)

- to grow in your understanding of God and His Word
  (1 Corinthians 2:14–15)

- to live a life pleasing to God (Galatians 5:16–23)

Remember the Promise of Jesus:

"But you will receive power when the Holy Spirit comes on you; and you will be my witnesses in Jerusalem, and in all Judea and Samaria, and to the ends of the earth" (Acts 1:8 NIV).

If you would like additional resources on the Holy Spirit, please go to www.nlpdirect.com.

Adapted from *Have You Made the Wonderful Discovery of the Spirit-filled Life?* written by Bill Bright, copyright © 1966. Published by New*Life* Publications, P.O. Box 593684, Orlando, FL 32859.

If this information has been of help to you, complete this page and send for free literature that has been designed for your spiritual growth.

___ I have received Jesus Christ as my Savior and Lord.

___ I am a Christian, and I would like further help in getting to know Christ better.

___ I still have questions. Please send me more information about Jesus Christ.

NAME

_____

ADDRESS

_____

CITY, STATE, ZIP

_____

Place in an envelope and mail to:

CAMPUS CRUSADE FOR CHRIST INTERNATIONAL
100 Sunport Lane, Dept. 2100
Orlando, FL 32809

NOTES

Chapter 1

1. "In the world you will have tribulation; but be of good cheer, I have overcome the world" (John 16:33 NKJV). "I am the resurrection and the life. He who believes in Me, though he may die, yet he shall live. And whoever lives and believes in Me shall never die" (John 11:25–26 NKJV).
2. Helen Nearing, *Light on Aging and Dying: Wise Words Selected by Helen Nearing,* (Thorndike, Maine: G. K. Hall & Co., 1995).

Chapter 2

1. Romans 8:38.
2. Psalm 23:4; 2 Timothy 1:7.
3. "Without faith it is impossible to please Him" (Heb. 11:6 NKJV). "So that's why faith is the key! God's promise is given to us as a free gift. And we are certain to receive it, whether or not we follow Jewish customs, if we have faith like Abraham's" (Rom. 4:16). "Whatever is not from faith is sin" (Rom. 14:23 NASB). "For therein is the righteousness of God revealed from faith to faith: as it is written, 'The just shall live by faith'" (Rom. 1:17 KJV).
4. Herbert Lockyer, *Last Words of Saints and Sinners* (Grand Rapids: Kriegel Publications, 1969), 131, 133.
5. Ibid., 58, 62–63, 65, 97–98.
6. "The Hubble Space Telescope Has Found There May Be 125 Billion Galaxies in the Universe," *South China Morning Post*, 9 January 1999.

Chapter 3

1. Fox Television News, 19 August 2002.

2. "All praise to the God and Father of our Lord Jesus Christ. He is the source of every mercy and the God who comforts us. He comforts us in all our troubles so that we can comfort others. When others are troubled, we will be able to give them the same comfort God has given us. You can be sure that the more we suffer for Christ, the more God will shower us with his comfort through Christ. So when we are weighed down with troubles, it is for your benefit and salvation! For when God comforts us, it is so that we, in turn, can be an encouragement to you. Then you can patiently endure the same things we suffer. We are confident that as you share in suffering, you will also share God's comfort. I think you ought to know, dear brothers and sisters, about the trouble we went through in the province of Asia. We were crushed and completely overwhelmed, and we thought we would never live through it. In fact, we expected to die. But as a result, we learned not to rely on ourselves, but on God who can raise the dead. And he did deliver us from mortal danger. And we are confident that he will continue to deliver us. He will rescue us because you are helping by praying for us. As a result, many will give thanks to God because so many people's prayers for our safety have been answered" (2 Cor. 1:3–11).

3. C. S. Lewis, *The Problem of Pain* (San Francisco: Harper San Francisco, 2001), 45.

Chapter 4

1. "This is what God has testified: He has given us eternal life, and this life is in his Son. So whoever has God's Son has life, whoever does not have his Son does not have life. I write this to you who believe in the Son of God that you may know you have eternal life" (1 John 5:11–13). Also: "If you confess with your mouth that Jesus is Lord and believe in your heart that God raised him from the dead, you will be saved. For it is by believing in your heart that you are made right with God, and it is by confessing with your mouth that you are saved. As the Scriptures tell us, 'Anyone who believes in him will not be disappointed.' Jew and Gentile are the same in this respect. They all have the same Lord, who generously gives his riches to all who ask for them. For 'anyone who calls on the name of the Lord will be saved'" (Rom. 10:9–13).

Chapter 6

1. Andrae Crouch, "Through It All," Manna Music Corp., 1971.

Chapter 7

1. Elbert Hubbard, *The Roycroft Dictionary and Epigrams,* quoted in the *Giant Book of American Quotations,* (Carruth and Ehrlich Books, Inc. 1988, Gramercy Books;

1999 edition Random House by agreement with HarperCollins Publishers, New York City).

2. James G. Lawson, *Deeper Experiences of Famous Christians* (New Kensington, Pa.: Whitaker House, 1998), 261.

Chapter 8

1. "I know I am rotten through and through so far as my old sinful nature is concerned. No matter which way I turn, I can't make myself do right. I want to, but I can't. When I want to do good, I don't. And when I try not to do wrong, I do it anyway. But if I am doing what I don't want to do, I am not really the one doing it; the sin within me is doing it. It seems to be a fact of life that when I want to do what is right, I inevitably do what is wrong. I love God's law with all my heart. But there is another law at work within me that is at war with my mind. This law wins the fight and makes me a slave to the sin that is still within me. Oh, what a miserable person I am. Who will free me from this life that is dominated by sin? Thank God! The answer is in Jesus Christ our Lord. So you see how it is: In my mind I really want to obey God's law, but because of my sinful nature I am a slave to sin. So now there is no condemnation for those who belong to Christ Jesus. For the power of the life-giving Spirit has freed you through Christ Jesus from the power of sin that leads to death" (Rom. 7:18–8:2).

2. Elizabeth C. Clephane, "Beneath the Cross of Jesus," public domain.

3. "So since God's grace has set us free from the law, does this mean we can go on sinning? Of course not! Don't you realize that whatever you choose to obey becomes your master? You can choose sin, which leads to death, or you can choose to obey God and receive his approval. Thank God! Once you were slaves of sin, but now you have obeyed with all your heart the new teaching God has given you. Now you are free from sin, your old master, and you have become slaves to your new master, righteousness. I speak this way, using the illustration of slaves and masters, because it is easy to understand. Before, you let yourselves be slaves of impurity and lawlessness. Now you must choose to be slaves of righteousness so that you will become holy. In those days, when you were slaves of sin, you weren't concerned with doing what was right. And what was the result? It was not good, since now you are ashamed of the things you used to do, things that end in eternal doom. But now you are free from the power of sin and have become slaves of God. Now you do those things that lead to holiness and result in eternal life. For the wages of sin is death, but the free gift of God is eternal life through Christ Jesus our Lord" (Rom. 6:15–23).

Chapter 9

1. William Booth. Biography. See http://psalm121.ca/quotes/dcqbooth.html
2. V. Raymond Edman, *The Disciplines of Life* (Minneapolis: World Wide Publications, 1948), 51.

Chapter 10

1. Dennis Medina, Eisenhower Museum and Public Library, 23 March 2003.

Chapter 11

1. S. Allen Foster, *Dying with Grace and Hope* (Palm Beach, Fla.: Desert Ministries, Inc. 1999), 28.
2. William J. Federer, *America's God and Country Encyclopedia of Quotations.*

Chapter 12

1. Bill Bright, *Jesus and the Intellectual,* 1968.
2. Josh McDowell, *Evidence That Demands a Verdict* (1992).
3. Paul Little, *Know Why You Believe* (Downers Grove, Ill.: InterVarsity Press, 1989).
4. McDowell, *Evidence That Demands a Verdict,* 82/4–6.
5. Ibid., 56/A–10.
6. For more on this see Josh D. McDowell, *The New Evidence That Demands a Verdict,* (Thomas Nelson, Inc. Publishers, Nashville) 204–84; a substantial portion of which was originally published by Here's Life Publishers, Inc., San Bernardino, Ca. © 1972, 1975, 1979, 1981, Campus Crusade for Christ Inc.
7. Richards, Lawrence, *New International Encyclopedia of Bible Words,* (Zondervan Corp. Grand Rapids, 1995), 136.
8. The Westminster Confession, 32.

Chapter 13

1. Charles Spurgeon, "C. H. Spurgeon's Prayers," cited in *Facing Forever* (Wake Forest, N.C.: Church Initiative, 2001), 29.
2. Wayne Grudem, *Bible Doctrines: Essential Teachings of the Christian Faith* (Grand Rapids: Zondervan, 1999), 176, 459.
3. Jonathan Edwards, quoted by Edward William Fudge, *The Fire That Consumes* (Houston: Providential Press, 1982), 417.

WILLIAM R. BRIGHT
1921–2003

Founder, Chairman, and President Emeritus,
Campus Crusade for Christ International

From a small beginning in 1951, the organization he began now has a presence in 196 countries in areas representing 99.6 percent of the world's population. Campus Crusade for Christ has more than 70 ministries and major projects, involving more than 25,000 full-time and 225,000 trained volunteer staff. Each ministry is designed to help fulfill the Great Commission, Christ's command to help carry the gospel of God's love and forgiveness in Christ to every person on earth.

Born in Coweta, Oklahoma, on October 19, 1921, Bright graduated with honors from Northeastern State University and completed five years of graduate study at Princeton and Fuller Theological Seminaries. He was awarded eight honorary doctorates from prestigious institutions and received numerous other recognitions, including the ECPA Gold Medallion Lifetime Achievement Award (2001), the Golden Angel Award as International Churchman of the Year (1982), and the $1.1 million Templeton Prize for Progress in Religion (1996), which he dedicated to promoting fasting and prayer throughout the world. He received the first-ever Lifetime Achievement Award from his alma mater (2001).

Bright authored more than 100 books, booklets, videos, and audio tapes, as well as thousands of articles and pamphlets, some of which have been printed in most major languages and distributed by the millions. Among his books are: *Come Help Change the World; The Secret; The Holy*

Spirit; A Man Without Equal; Life Without Equal; The Coming Revival; The Transforming Power of Fasting & Prayer; Red Sky in the Morning (coauthor); *GOD: Discover His Character; Living Supernaturally in Christ;* and the booklet *Have You Heard of the Four Spiritual Laws?* (which has an estimated 2.5 billion circulation).

He was also responsible for many individual initiatives in ministry, particularly in evangelism. For example, the *JESUS* film, which he conceived and financed through Campus Crusade, has, by latest estimates, been viewed by over 5.5 billion people in 236 nations and provinces. In the past year he led in the founding of the Global Pastors Network with a goal of establishing 5 million house churches worldwide and training pastors via electronic media, and he launched the "Discover God" movement.

His wife, Vonette, who assisted him in founding Campus Crusade for Christ, resides in Orlando, Florida, as do their son Brad and his wife, Katherine, with two children. Their son Zac and his wife, Terry, and their two children reside in California, where he is a Presbyterian pastor and leader in the California C. S. Lewis Society.